Najiba

Psalm 67

John Weaver

Love is what makes life worth living! And this love story is unique, powerful, and fascinating. Five stars!

—**STEVEN EARP**

AUTHOR/PRODUCER, *WHERE WAS GOD?*

John and Jeanne's love story is extraordinary, an inspiration, and definitely a must read.

—**MEGAN BAKER**

SALES LEAD Q SCIENCES,

FORMER TOP LEADER AT LE-VEL

I'm so blessed by John's life and amazing love story from Afghanistan.

—**RASHAWN COPELAND**

DIRECTOR, *I'M SO BLESSED DAILY* &

WITHOUT WALLS MINISTRIES

An exciting memoir...*Najiba* is an awesome testimony and example of God's provision in our life and purpose in our marriage. Very intriguing!

—**GREG & JULIE GORMAN**

FOUNDERS, *MARRIED FOR A PURPOSE*

I highly recommend John and Jeanne's inspiring love story from Afghanistan.

—**KATE MCCORD**

AUTHOR, *THE LAND OF BLUE BURQAS*

I've known John since college—his adventures are a modern-day marvel—but who knew he'd find a wife like Jeanne! This is the Lord's doing and it's marvelous. There's risk and romance on every page. You'll absolutely enjoy it.

—**ROBERT J. MORGAN**
BEST SELLING AUTHOR, PASTOR, SPEAKER

See how God orchestrates us meeting certain people to change eternity in this incredible journey.

—**CASEY JONES**
DIRECTOR, *AMERICAN DREAM CENTER*

This will captivate you as two souls converge by divine design in the midst of epic world events.

—**DR. SID WEBB**
FOUNDER, *BUILD WHAT COUNTS*
& *SHARPENED FOCUS*

John and Jeanne's lives are a wonderful example of what God can do in and through those who obey Him.

—**BRENDA LEE ABRAM NAKAMURA**
FOUNDER, *SINGLE TO MARRIED GOD'S WAY*

Filled with intrigue, laughter, suspense, and romance of a couple whose hearts have been ignited with an uncommon love for the people of Afghanistan.

—**JEFF REED**
PRODUCER, *AMERICAN FAMILY ASSOCIATION*

Najiba

A Love Story from Afghanistan
John Weaver with Jeanette Windle

Copyright © 2019 by John Weaver

Weaver United

ISBN 978-1-7330011-0-6 (print book)
ISBN 978-1 -7330011-1-3 (e-book)

Visit Author at **facebook.com/weaverunited**
Cover Design by Brittany Edsall and Dan Barry at **www.smallmedialarge.org**
Book and E-Book designed and formatted by **www.ebooklistingservices.com**

PROLOGUE

WHERE WERE YOU ON September 11, 2001? If you are old enough to remember that horrific day, then you know exactly where you were. I was in Afghanistan.

What was I doing in Afghanistan on 9/11? Perhaps you heard some of the story on ABC's *World News Tonight* with Peter Jennings or on CNN with Sarai Shah. Or maybe you've read one of my previous books, *Inside Afghanistan* or *A Flame on the Front Line*.

How about May 24, 2005? Do you remember where you were? For most people it was an ordinary day, not one you'd recall without checking the calendar. Yet in Afghanistan history was being made as I married my lovely bride Jeanne, or *Najiba* as she is known there.

Our wedding was historic for several reasons. First, I'd been engaged twice before, but after two strikes I finally hit the perfect home run. Second, as far as we know, it was the first wedding ceremony celebrated on Afghan soil where the Gospel (Good News) of Jesus Christ was proclaimed to hundreds of Afghans in their own language. Third, even though our holy matrimony was clearly Christ-centered, the Islamic Republic of Afghanistan officially certified our marriage certificate.

Yes, the 24th of May was a phenomenal day. Of course, there is nothing remarkable about us. But God is great! Our Everlasting Father is awesome—the God of wonders. Even to this day, Afghans still talk about the extraordinary miracles of our wedding week.

Among those miracles is how Almighty God ordained our union for His glory. An arranged marriage is not hard to find in Afghanistan. Over the centuries, millions of nuptials have been prearranged in that part of the planet. But finding a passionate, sacrificial love story is not as easy.

With the blessing and permission of our parents, we wed because of our shared attraction and affection for each other. We also know our Heavenly Father brought us together in ways that can only be described as divine orchestration. We've been asked numerous times whether our marriage was prearranged or based on mutual love. Our answer is, "Yes, it is both." Our marital vows were birthed from destiny and desire.

Jeanne and I call it an arranged-love marriage. The Sovereign Lord led us to each other as He set up our love-at-first-sight encounter in Kabul, the capital of Afghanistan. This was a delightful surprise to us. Now we see the Hand of Providence in every step from our initial meeting to months of long-distance courtship to boldly saying "I do" surrounded by hundreds of Afghans.

We fell in love, not by random chance or forced choice, but based on God's unique design and ultimate purpose for our lives. On May 24, 2005, we willingly entered a covenant together as husband and wife, committing our lives to each other till death do us part. A promise that reflects, however dimly, the Lord's redeeming love for us.

I praise God for giving me my princess bride and for the privilege of being her bridegroom. In the simplest terms, we are God's gift of grace to each other. "You are my full blessing," we often remind one another. I'm still learning that God has greater plans for bringing us together than just our own benefit. Through our relationship and even our children, God has been writing another chapter of *His-Story.*

Since the epic events of our weeklong wedding celebrations, we've been asked a thousand times to write a book about our marriage in the mysterious land of the Afghans. The following pages contain as much as we can put into words. For security reasons, some details have been redacted and names changed. Yet from cover to cover you'll find a fascinating, inspiring, and unforgettable romance bursting with adventure, drama, and suspense. You may also discover that our incredible story pales in comparison to the greatest love story of all.

1: JOHN

SPRING HAD ARRIVED with singing birds and budding flowers in Feyzabad, the capital of Badakhshan. Nestled among the massive Hindu Kush mountain range in northeastern Afghanistan, the river valley known as the "land of grace" was gradually warming to green after a long, snowy winter. The fragrance of lamb *palau* served earlier to over a thousand residents still mingled with the dust of unpaved streets and the fresh scent of a light drizzle. In an hour my bride would emerge from a side door piercing the mud-brick wall that separated my own living quarters from the neighboring compound where female members of the bridal party were being hosted.

At thirty-five years of age with two failed engagements, I was about to marry the most beautiful woman in Afghanistan. Though how would I really know since almost all the Afghan women I saw were fully covered in burkas? Nevertheless, Najiba was the one our Heavenly Father had chosen and prepared for me in ways so unbelievable I still held my breath lest I wake up and discover it had all been a dream. Even more significant, our wedding would be the first public Christ-centered ceremony to be conducted here, an event that would have been impossible under Taliban rule.

Definitely, this was the divine day the Lord had made. Yet where my heart should have been overflowing with joy, I felt stark terror instead. I, who had lived for years as a flame on the front line, dismissing and even reveling in the adrenaline of routine danger, was now scared to death.

The morning had been full of preparations, followed by hosting the city's VIPs (Very Important Persons) and a good portion of Feyzabad's male residents for the traditional prenuptial midday feast in the bridegroom's home. My "home" was actually the compound that served as the northeastern headquarters of our aid organization. By now, our lunch guests had mostly left. Hundreds would return for the official ceremony itself. I relinquished the remaining wedding preparations to make my own ablutions. My beloved would be absolutely irresistible and altogether lovely. The least I could do was present her with a clean, freshly-dressed bridegroom.

The compound was a typical Afghan residence, a rectangular walled courtyard with a two-story, eight-room main dwelling at one end and several one-story rooms running across the other end. Along the interior wall was the small wooden door that connected this compound with the one housing my bride. Halfway along the exterior wall was the main gate into the property.

Like most residences, there was no indoor plumbing, much less a shower or bath. Instead of a fancy Western-style tuxedo, I gathered up the specially-tailored, white-gold *shalwar kameez* I'd be wearing as the bridegroom, then headed across the courtyard into a small side room designated as a washroom. Awaiting me was a bucket of clean water, soap, and shampoo. My weekly birdbath, as my mother would call it.

I'd barely started washing when panic hit me. This was no ordinary pre-wedding jitters—not that I had a lot of prior experience! My heart was racing so hard it felt as though it might explode. I was shaking like a leaf. Overwhelmed and paralyzed with fear, I couldn't even lift a sponge to wash.

Inside my mind, confusing doubts and condemning interrogations tormented me. *Are you crazy? What are you doing? You've already failed twice! Who are you to marry such an exceptional lady? She is out of your league! She hardly knows you. And what do you really know about her?*

The penetrating voices had a point. In the months since first meeting in Kabul, Jeanne and I had been in each other's company only a handful of days. We had never kissed or even held hands. I'd barely seen her hair since she always wore a head covering. Yet we'd soon be alone as husband and wife in an Afghan bridal chamber specially prepared for us.

And what about the wedding itself? This was a conservative Muslim area. Most all the Afghans around us knew I was a completely committed follower of Jesus. The town elders and VIPs had given us permission to hold our wedding here—perhaps out of friendship, respect, and gratitude for our years of service to the Afghan people. Many were also curious to see a wedding of two Christ-followers. Some were drawn by the word on the street that this wasn't a marriage where the bride might meet her bridegroom for the first time, but a love match.

The local elders might not have consented so easily had they known we'd use loudspeakers to unashamedly declare the Gospel. Had I been wrong in my belief that God was leading me to do just that? Was I instead putting my bride-to-be at risk of retaliation from possible extremists?

The haunting voices were still echoing. By now I was crouched down, hardly able to breathe from anxiety. *Lord Jesus, help me!* I prayed, remembering my Savior's own agonizing experience and anguished prayer in the garden of Gethsemane. *Jesus, please come rescue me! Deliver me from evil. Take this away! Please save me!*

The internal turmoil suddenly became a roaring blast. Immediately, I recognized this wasn't just my own inner struggle, but a satanic attack. A piercing voice screamed into my mind. *You can't do this! This is MY territory! You aren't going to hold a Christ-centered wedding here and broadcast my enemy's Gospel message on a loudspeaker for everyone to hear.*

At that moment, I wasn't thinking of the prophet Daniel's intercession with God, which had lasted three weeks before the archangels Gabriel and Michael were able to defeat the demonic prince of Persia and deliver God's answer (Daniel 10). Later it did occur to me that, like Daniel, I too stood in the ancient land of Persia. And Satan's appointed prince of this territory certainly didn't want the witness of Jesus Christ (*Isa al-Musih*) infiltrating his stronghold.

There is a well-known proverb: what God has shown you in the light, don't doubt in the darkness. Still feeling intimidated and with a sense of trepidation, I made a conscious choice to focus my mind on God's truth and what He had shown me. I knew God had called me and sent me here to be His servant. I also knew God had brought Najiba, the virtuous woman waiting on the other side of the wall, into my life to be my wife.

I was also reminded of the reality of my own shortcomings and past mistakes. I was far from perfect. I'd failed in other relationships. Nevertheless, God had clearly shown me and confirmed it through many others that it was His good and pleasing will for me to marry Najiba. After all, she'd said "yes" and her parents had given permission.

Even more so, we both had complete assurance from God that our wedding was to be a witness to the Afghan people. For such a time as this, we were God's flames on the front line. This was not just about John wooing and winning his bride, but about the greatest love story of all.

How long that spiritual battle actually lasted, only God knows. I remember confessing my sins, crying out words of Holy Scripture, rebuking the powers of darkness in the name of the Lord, beseeching the Prince of Peace for His presence, peace, power, and protection over all of us, and singing victoriously the famed Martin Luther hymn, *A Mighty Fortress Is Our God.*

Were there unseen angels warring against the prince of Persia himself or the evil forces around me? I don't know. I do remember how the Spirit of God came over me, casting out all my fears, creating in me a clean heart, and causing me to arise with fresh faith and renewed vision.

Filled with overwhelming peace and strength beyond my own, I finished bathing and dressing. I felt supernaturally cleansed from head to toe on the inside as well as on the outside. Rekindled passion stirred and blazed inside me, not just for my own bride, but for the Beloved Bridegroom, King Jesus. I longed to boldly proclaim His Word that burned within me and to see His glory made known among the Afghan people.

Refreshed, revived, and ready, I walked out of the washroom to receive my bride.

2: JOHN

I REACHED THE LAND of my dreams in August 2000, ready to give my life to serve those suffering. The need was tremendous since the tyranny of the Taliban had produced millions of IDPs (internally displaced persons), compounded by a nationwide drought and a series of crippling earthquakes in northern Afghanistan. God had opened the door for me to join an international organization that offered emergency relief and community development programs.

Before 9/11 few outside its borders knew much about Afghanistan except its status as one of the planet's poorest countries, which included one of the lowest life expectancies and highest infant mortality rates. Some might remember the U.S.-backed war of resistance against Soviet occupation in the 1980s, which culminated not just in Russia's withdrawal from Afghanistan in 1989, but the crumbling of the entire Soviet Union, an outcome for which Afghan freedom fighters still like to take credit.

Less publicized was the ensuing spiral into chaos that had morphed into a civil war between the mujahedeen factions who had once united to help drive out the Soviets. Their conflict was less about the differing ideologies each side claimed and more about ethnicity, language, tribal identity, and historic hostility.

On one side were the Pashtuns of eastern and southern Afghanistan, who owed allegiance more to their tribal brothers in Pakistan, from whom they'd been split by an arbitrary boundary set during British colonial rule. On the other side was the so-called Northern Alliance of Tajiks, Uzbeks, Hazaras, and others whose trade language, Dari, had more in common with Iran or Tajikistan than its eastern neighbors.

By the time I arrived, the Pashtun-dominated fundamentalist coalition known as the Taliban had not only seized control of Kabul, but up to eighty percent of Afghanistan's territory. This left the Northern Alliance as an embattled resistance force based mostly in the northeastern mountain region of Badakhshan. The other major Northern Alliance stronghold was in the Panjshir, home of the famous General Ahmad Shah Massoud, who was killed by a suicide attack on September 9, 2001, just a few kilometers from one of our IDP camps.

Assisted by Al-Qaeda and other radical factions, the Taliban's brutal regime, along with years of ethnic fighting, had left in ruins a countryside already decimated by a decade of conflict with the Russians. This created a refugee crisis that left six million out of the country's thirty million exiled in Pakistan, Iran, and other nations as well as more than a million displaced internally.

Little of this was making international news before the terrorist attacks on September 11, 2001. Of more interest was the whereabouts of Sheik Osama bin Laden, the one-time United States ally in training and arming the Afghan mujahedeen against the Soviets, now among America's most-wanted for attacks both inside and outside the United States, including the 1998 assaults on U.S. embassies in Kenya and Tanzania. By this time, Osama bin Laden and his organization, Al-Qaeda, had found sanctuary inside Afghanistan, courtesy of his comrades, the Taliban.

The outside world knew very little about the various humanitarian organizations serving Afghans during this crisis. Apart from my family, close friends, and co-workers, no one knew about a new American aid worker named John Weaver. This was fine with me as remaining under the radar isn't only protocol but common sense for a passionate follower of Jesus Christ working in strict Islamic territory.

By 2001, I'd been appointed regional program manager of our humanitarian efforts, which included disaster response, emergency relief, food-for-work programs, and various reconstruction projects. The days were long, and the demands were high. Yet God was using us to make an impact and to improve the quality of life for thousands of hopeless and hurting Afghans.

Then the horrific events of September 11th shook our world. I was in Feyzabad when I first received news of Al-Qaeda's attack on the Twin Towers and the Pentagon. My account of how God allowed me to be one of the few Americans on the Afghan side of the Amu Darya River when the United States-Northern Alliance joint invasion force rolled through to overthrow the Taliban can be found in my first book, *Inside Afghanistan*.

After 9/11, news agencies flooded to northern Afghanistan via Tajikistan on the heels of the U.S. military invasion. Most were surprised to learn of an American aid worker in the area. In October 2001, while getting some supplies in a local bazaar, a former student working as a translator for NBC spotted me through the crowd. He tried to introduce me to various reporters. At first glance they didn't believe I was the American aid worker they'd heard about since I looked like an Afghan.

Due to possible security risks, I needed to obtain permission from my superiors before sharing too much with the media. After being told to proceed with caution, I reluctantly agreed to be interviewed. Soon the news of our humanitarian work was circulating worldwide via ABC, CNN, *The New Yorker*, the Associated Press, *The Boston Globe*, *Yahoo News*, NBC, Reuters, *The News and Observer*, *The Daily Record*, and many more news agencies.

Without any desire, effort, or planning of my own, I gained a public international exposure that God used in a good way. I became a voice to those concerned as well as a window for many to see inside Afghanistan. Yes, for a short period 9/11 and its repercussions put an ordinary aid worker in the spotlight. More importantly, it put Afghanistan on everyone's map.

My unsolicited five minutes of fame would unexpectedly necessitate a trip to the United States in December 2001. Strangely, while dozing off on the long plane ride, I had a reoccurring dream about writing a book. It was so vivid that I woke up to write down specific images, themes, and even chapter titles.

While in the U.S., I was given several opportunities to speak about Afghanistan, one of which led to being asked if I'd consider writing a book about my experience. Recalling my dream on the plane, I knew God was up to something. Shortly after, the book project *Inside Afghanistan* was born.

I soon found myself traveling throughout North America and other countries to share my story. I was also asked to speak on TV and radio interviews as well as at civic and church gatherings. Many more news articles and books were written as this war-torn, mostly overlooked corner of the earth became the focus of global attention.

More significantly, the land of the Afghans was now in the eyes and hearts of God's people. All over the globe, churches, ministries, and the faith-based community were praying for Afghanistan. It looked like God was using what was intended for evil for greater good.

The Taliban had been ousted. Organizations and aid workers began pouring into Afghanistan to help rebuild and restore lives. They came not just from the U.S. or other western nations, but from all over God's creation. At a non-governmental organization (NGO) gathering a few years after 9/11, I counted more than fifty nationalities.

Because of my exposure and experience, some of these workers contacted me. Along with my regional responsibilities, my influence expanded to one of a countrywide connector between several organizations. I saw this as God's Kingdom of love and peace expanding. It was a role I thrived in and enjoyed.

Many of the fears and problems from years of civil war had given way to hope for the future. Here was a unique opportunity, not just for Afghanistan but for the rest of the world too. Much good has been accomplished since

9/11. But this newfound optimism wouldn't last as news headlines over the last several years have made clear.

Yet back in 2002, the possibilities seemed limitless. The central government and international military presence promised restored stability and security. The global community had designated billions of dollars for infrastructure and reconstruction, which would facilitate community development and rehabilitation projects. Schools were reopening. Hospitals were being rebuilt. Opportunities were flourishing, even for women and girls. Education and practical skills training were abounding around the country.

I was excited to move beyond emergency relief projects. There is a time to help people temporarily survive, but it is long-term, sustainable community development programs that bring lasting transformation. I'd always loved the proverb: "Give a man a fish and you feed him for one day. Teach a man to fish and you feed him for a lifetime."

God had given us a vision for an educational training center. To this point, that vision had been overshadowed by necessary emergency disaster response activities. Still, in an act of faith shortly before 9/11, we'd rented a compound not far from our office. Our plan was to offer English, computer, and health courses for men and women as well as teacher training initiatives.

On a trip to the U.S., I had the privilege of transporting twelve laptop computers back to Feyzabad. Our team's IT specialist connected them to our solar-powered satellite dish to provide the first functioning wireless network and internet services in northeastern Afghanistan. Every day, this project equipped and empowered local Afghan men and women so they in turn could teach and train their own communities.

I was excited about another experience—openness. The prayers being poured out around the world for Afghanistan were evident. This was still a conservative Islamic setting, but with the Taliban out of power, people felt more open to express curiosity.

"Why did you come here?" Afghans would often ask me.

"Almighty God sent me here to serve," I responded simply. If they probed, I'd continue, "When Jesus lived on earth, He demonstrated God's unconditional love by feeding the hungry, helping the poor, healing the sick, and sharing God's life-giving Word. I am here to show that same incredible and indescribable love of God."

As a Christ-follower in an extremely hostile environment, I had to tread carefully. Jesus told His disciples, "I send you out as sheep in the midst of wolves. Therefore be wise as serpents and harmless as doves" (Matthew 10:16 NKJV).

Especially since the ousting of the Taliban didn't bring freedom of religion and speech. Responding to a question was no problem. On the other hand, openly evangelizing, distributing Bibles, or holding church services were still criminal offenses.

Yet who can stop the Lord Almighty? No one! God is great, and nothing can keep Him from advancing His Kingdom that endures throughout all generations. Yes, the Spirit of God was moving mightily. The Beloved Bridegroom was wooing His bride, drawing people to Himself all across the Islamic world. Repeatedly, we heard stories of Muslims meeting Isa al-Masih (Jesus

Christ) in dreams and visions. Often our friends would inquire to know more about the Prince of Peace and His teachings because of some supernatural encounter, revelation, or miracle.

God's Word was spreading in other ways. One day I was requested to serve as an international monitor for the World Health Organization (WHO), which was carrying out a vaccination campaign. I didn't want to participate. I'd been putting in long hours and was exhausted. Moreover, medicine wasn't my area of expertise. Surely the WHO team could find someone more qualified. Besides, I had a tendency to pass out at the sight of blood. Nevertheless, WHO persisted, and out of a sense of duty, I finally agreed.

By the time we reached the end of an awfully dusty, bouncy, unpaved road, I asked myself again, *What on earth am I doing here?* The vaccination campaign was in one of the village's mudbrick buildings. Parents were lining up outside with their children. There was always a crowd of people around me until the noonday break, when I found myself having lunch with the Afghan doctor in charge of the campaign. Glancing around, he suddenly leaned forward to ask quietly, "So did you hear the radio program last night?"

I had no idea what he was talking about. Voice of America? BBC? Tiredly, I responded, "No, I wasn't listening to the radio last night."

As the doctor continued, I wasn't really paying attention until I caught a reference to "Words of Life." Then I realized he was talking about a specific radio program I'd listened to many times before, but last night I'd been too busy. The doctor explained how the program had spoken of living water that Jesus Christ promised to those who follow Him. Looking directly at me, he asked, "Can you tell me what this means?"

I was now fully attentive. Feeling like the disciple of Christ, Philip, when he miraculously encountered the Ethiopian eunuch in the book of Acts, chapter eight, I responded to his thirst for living water. I also breathed a repentant prayer, *Father God, please forgive me for not wanting to be involved in this campaign. I can see clearly now that You sent me here. You are sovereign and You are at work here!*

Another day, I met an Afghan man who was a returning refugee from a neighboring country. He asked a lot of questions. Then to my astonishment, he leaned in and said, "May I tell you how I came to know the Messiah?"

As God continued to bring such divine appointments and ministry moments into my life, He gave me a reoccurring vision of thousands of lighthouses blazing all across Afghanistan. I'd come to love this land and its people dearly. My heart was also filled with faith that God had many children here. Feyzabad means "place of grace." And by God's amazing grace and for His greater glory, I hoped to serve and share His life-changing love story for many years in my new home town.

But as excited as I was to be back and to further advance God's Kingdom, I still had one aching hole in my life.

3: JEANNE

ONE QUESTION I'M OFTEN asked is how I ended up with Kabul, Afghanistan, listed as place of birth on my passport. Perhaps the best answer is that my parents, Jim and Jane Bonner, were far from a typical American couple. Both were Foreign Service personnel with the U.S Department of State when they met in Eritrea, Africa, which was then part of Ethiopia under Emperor Haile Selassie. My father was an engineer and my mother a linguist.

Decades later my parents fell in love while working in Africa. They got engaged while on safari at the foot of Mt. Kilimanjaro in Kenya. In 1968, they married in Asmara, the capital of Eritrea, without either set of parents present. Decades later, my mother assured me they would not be upset if I married a man they hadn't yet met since they'd done precisely the same to their parents. After their wedding, my parents spent their honeymoon at the source of the Blue Nile River in Ethiopia. The following year, my older brother Steve was born in Asmara.

Their next adventure led them to work at the American Embassy in Kabul, Afghanistan. In the spring of 1972, my mother gave birth to me, her only daughter. I have no childhood memories of Kabul since I was only three months old when my parents relocated to a new post in Germany.

My first real memories began in Thailand, where we moved when I was almost four years old. One day in Bangkok, my brother and I asked my parents why we were Americans. After all, we'd never lived in the USA, nor were we born there. My mother, at first stumped by the question, answered, "Because you have American passports."

I was in the first grade when my parents were assigned to a posting in Washington, D.C. My initial adjustment to American culture wasn't easy. I remember one classmate calling me a traitor because I'd been born in Afghanistan, which was under Soviet occupation at that time. I came home in tears.

"You've got to stand your ground and not let anyone push you around," my mother told me. "Go back and tell that boy how America has helped Afghanistan and that he doesn't know what he's talking about!"

Hands on my hips, I sought out my classmate the next day at school and did just that. It was one lesson my mom taught me that has served me well ever since. Wherever God puts you in life, be strong, stand firm, and don't be afraid to speak the truth.

My mother was raised Catholic and my father Methodist. I recall going to Sunday school while I was a small child in Germany and Thailand. I remember my mother teaching us about God, in part because there were Buddhist temples and statues of Buddha everywhere in Thailand. When we saw people bowing to the images, she'd tell my brother and me, "Those are their gods. We have our own God, so we don't bow down to or worship their idols."

Once we settled in Northern Virginia, we began attending a small Presbyterian church. The services confirmed my own awareness that there was a God in heaven who'd created me and called me to worship Him. I loved Sunday school, especially when I learned that my name, Jeanne, means "God is gracious." Later in life, I would discover that Jeanne and Jane, my mother's name, are both feminine variants of the biblical name John.

My first memory of answered prayer occurred when I was eight years old. Each year, all the Sunday school students who reached third grade were given a brand-new Bible. I was full of excitement and anticipation to reach that spiritual milestone. But just before the Bible presentation ceremony, I learned we'd be moving again. I began praying that God would delay our next move so I could get that special Bible. I don't remember all the details, but my parents' assignment in the U.S. was extended, so I did receive my first Bible.

I still have that Bible. Though the writing has faded, I can still read the inscription on the front: Jeanne Louise Donner, 1981, March 22nd. At the Bible presentation, I also received some stickers, including a gilt crown. I carefully placed these on the Bible in acknowledgement that I was crowning Jesus Christ as the King of my life. Although my faith in God was quite childlike, I had absolute assurance that God had answered my prayers and that He was pleased with this simple act of obedience.

My brother and I had begun to adjust to American life and culture—just in time for my parents' next posting in Greece. For fifth grade, I attended an international school in Athens. Then we moved to Rome for my sixth and seventh grades. My family didn't go to church in either country.

But something within me—whether curiosity, an urging of the Holy Spirit, or both—compelled me to pick up my Bible. I read it like any other book, starting in the beginning with Genesis, then Exodus, working my way through to Leviticus and Numbers or some other difficult passage before giving up. Months later, I'd pick it up and start over, making it as far as Deuteronomy or Joshua before stopping again.

In Rome, two other books greatly influenced me. The stories were life testimonies of girls who'd come to Christ through the ministry of the Walter Hoving Home (WHH), a Teen Challenge center for young women. A Bible-based recovery program for substance abusers, Teen Challenge was founded by renowned evangelist David Wilkerson, whose autobiographical account *The Cross and the Switchblade* had by this time been released in both book and movie format. David Wilkerson was also the founder of Times Square Church in New York City (NYC).

I could never have imagined as a young teenager the impact David Wilkerson would eventually have on me. At this point, I was struck by the dramatic transformation these girls had experienced at WHH. Even though my own life experience wasn't as blatantly disobedient or rebellious, I knew I too needed that kind of spiritual renewal.

At the end of each book was a prayer of repentance asking God for forgiveness of sins and acceptance into God's family in the name of the Lord Jesus Christ, who had died on the cross and risen again from the dead. I'd believed in God for several years. Yet at that moment I called on the Lord to save me by His blood, fill me with His Spirit, and change my life for His glory and purposes.

Now as I look back at my spiritual journey, I can see the Hand of God orchestrating each step. First, I learned about the one, true God from my parents while surrounded by idols in Thailand. Next came those Sunday school years in Virginia, where in answer to prayer I received my very first Bible. To this was added the inspiration I received from those WHH testimonies during the years of minimal spiritual exposure in Rome.

Another significant element of those years overseas can be attributed to my mother. While my father was often traveling on temporary duty assignments (TDY), my mother made it her mission to create a sense of "home" for us wherever we lived at the time. This included rounding up neighborhood kids to play with my brother and me.

Consequently, unlike the more sheltered upbringing of many Foreign Service kids, I was immediately immersed in the local culture and language everywhere we lived. By junior high, I'd added elementary Thai, Greek, and Italian to my native English, which instilled in me a love of learning new cultures and languages.

This fascinating life ended in eighth grade when my parents took another stateside posting. Attending a public high school in northern Virginia was the hardest culture shock I've experienced to this day, including Afghanistan. Half the time, I had no idea what the American teenagers around me were talking about. When they made fun of me, I reminded myself of my mother's advice to just stand my ground and refuse to be bullied.

I found my feet eventually, thanks to a devout Christian family living across the street, whose daughter Jessica became my best friend. While we didn't go to church as a family, various parents would pick me up to participate in youth group. What made an indelible impression on me was Jessica's mother, who always prayed for her daughter and me before we left their house and when we were sick. The concept of living life immersed in constant prayer intrigued me. Above all, the vibrant faith of my friend's mother showed me that God was listening to her prayers and desired His children to commune with Him.

Another positive aspect of those years was discovering that I enjoyed athletics, especially swimming. I joined my first swim team in Italy, and my first race in Rome remains a vivid memory. I dreaded embarrassing myself by coming in dead last. Sure enough, when I touched the wall at the end of the race and raised my head from the water, I discovered I was all alone. But before tears could start, swimmers in other lanes began closing in, and I realized that, far from dead last, I'd won the race.

Throughout high school, I swam competitively, and my teammates became my closest friends. Then just before my senior year, my parents received orders for another assignment in Thailand. I was devastated. Many of my teammates planned to attend college on swimming scholarships. How could I earn a scholarship if I completed my senior year in Thailand?

Thankfully, my parents knew of a prestigious boarding school, Pine Crest School in Fort Lauderdale, Florida, which offered rigorous academics coupled with an internationally-recognized swimming program. While my parents returned to Thailand, I finished my senior year at Pine Crest and absolutely loved it. The school also provided a shuttle bus for students who lived on campus to attend local churches. So on Sunday mornings and Wednesday nights, I attended Coral Ridge Presbyterian Church.

When I graduated in 1990, I did receive a swimming scholarship to North Carolina State University (NCSU). For the next four and a half years at NCSU, swimming took at least forty hours of my week on top of my studies. Gradually, church involvement or any real spiritual life fell by the wayside. Swimming had become my idol. Still, by the time I graduated with a major in Applied Mathematics and a minor in Computer Science, I realized that I was not Olympic material. So instead of pursuing a swimming career, I found a job as a computer systems administrator for an online think tank.

The following year, an opportunity opened up with a large management consulting firm. My job was to help businesses maximize their potential on the internet, still a new field in the 1990s. The workload was demanding, involving long hours and a lot of travel. Despite a busy schedule, I started going to church again with my high school friend Jessica, who was now married to a youth pastor.

The local congregation was small, but their passionate commitment to reach the unreached with Christ's transforming love, as well as the way the pastor taught God's Word, spoke directly to my heart. I was growing in my relationship with God. And for the first time, I felt I'd found a church home. Even though I knew I wasn't ready, I also believed God was telling me He had a plan for me to serve Him in ways that would take me beyond the borders of the USA.

In 1997, my consulting firm began sending me to New York City. I didn't want to go. My only visit to NYC in the late 1980s as a junior in high school had left me with the impression of a dark, dirty, crime-ridden city. Much of this was turned around under Mayor Rudy Giuliani's famous city cleanup in the 1990s. Still, one more crowded mega-city on the scale of Athens, Rome, Bangkok, or other such places where I'd lived was hardly my notion of a desirable living situation, much less a place I could ever call home.

How little did I know!

4: JOHN

AT THE BEGINNING OF TIME in the Garden of Eden, God created the first man, Adam, faultless—unlike me. God placed Adam in the perfect environment—unlike my own. God also provided for Adam's every possible need, including interaction with every animal species and daily fellowship with the Almighty Himself. Still, something was missing. Or should we say—someone?

In short, Adam was lonely. In Genesis, the first book of the Bible, God gives a major reason for creating a female counterpart: "It is not good for the man to be alone. I will make a helper suitable for him" (Genesis 2:18 NIV).

So God fashioned Eve, the first woman, from Adam's own DNA, flesh of his flesh, bone of his bone. Together, Adam (male) and Eve (female) completed and complemented each other. United as husband and wife and soon to be father and mother, they would more fully reflect the loving nature and relational character of God, the One who made them in His own image and for His own glory.

Back inside Afghanistan, I was now thirty-four years old and still single. If Adam with all that God had provided him could feel lonely without a wife to share his life, there could be nothing unspiritual in yearning for a bride of my own despite all the blessings God had showered upon me. Still, if Jesus was pursuing His Bride throughout Afghanistan, I sure wasn't meeting many promising candidates for myself.

This was in part because of the local culture. While Feyzabad presumably had as many female residents as male, the women were generally hidden under a *burqa*, the all-encompassing cover that for much of the world since 9/11 has become symbolic of Afghanistan. For cultural reasons, my NGO colleagues and friends were all male. They would never think of inviting me to see the uncovered faces of their female family members. Nor were there single women in my own age demographic among Feyzabad's small expatriate community.

Kabul was another story. Aid, government, military, and corporate organizations were flooding in by the thousands, either to offer a helping hand as volunteers or to capitalize on the top-dollar profits of the reconstruction bonanza. Although no longer as inaccessible as under Taliban rule, overland travel from Badakhshan to Kabul could still take several days, and air flights into Feyzabad's single, dilapidated Russian-era airstrip were rare.

More than that, despite a Master's Degree in Intercultural Studies, years of experience as an international aid worker, as well as being an author and public speaker, there was nothing really remarkable about me. I was just a simple guy who'd been spared a broken neck or a sojourn in jail only because of the mercy of Jesus Christ in my life. What God-fearing single female in the big city of Kabul would be interested in an ordinary mountain man like me or the amenity-lacking, remote village area where I lived?

Feyzabad sits in a valley at 1,254 meters in elevation, or approximately 4,000 feet, surrounded by rising folds of parched, beige foothills that merge into one of the planet's tallest mountain ranges, the Hindu Kush. In winter the town is snow-blown and freezing. In summer it is dust-blown and hot.

The saving grace of the region, the Kokcha River, flows right through the middle of Feyzabad. Or rather, the town runs along both sides of the Kokcha's winding curves. The river provides not only a water reserve but makes the valley a green oasis where various grains can be farmed along with vegetable gardens and orchards. This also makes the river banks prime real estate since, as with Egypt's Nile, the greenness peters out within a few kilometers from the river's edge into barren wasteland or beyond to massive, rocky mountains.

As mentioned, Feyzabad is the capital city of Badakhshan Province, which borders Tajikistan, Pakistan, and China. But at that time it was basically an overgrown mountain village with mostly unpaved streets and mudbrick houses. The only running water came from open canals and a single tap in each neighborhood that functioned on a rotating basis at the personal will of the mayor. Its shopping center was a row of metal-shuttered shops and an open-air bazaar.

There were some nicer areas. These places included buildings where former Northern Alliance warlords reigned as provincial governor, ministers, or other administrative positions parceled out to the winning side by the new central government. But all these finer facilities paled in comparison to most of Kabul, especially Wazir Akbar Khan, the upper-class neighborhood where Jeanne was born.

By this time, our NGO operation had expanded into a double compound, basically two adjacent mud-walled rectangles. Both rectangles had two-story residences side by side at one end, the first painted green and the other red. The red house also boasted a wide concrete veranda. A pedestrian gate in the central shared wall allowed passage between the two compounds. At the other end of both compounds were single-story individual rooms that opened onto the courtyard, some of them outhouses, washrooms, kitchen quarters, or storage units. A few fruit trees and flowering bushes offered a touch of green.

The furnishings were typical Afghan: rugs and long bolster pillows called *tushaks* for lounging or sleeping, along with tables, chairs, and shelving reserved largely for the computer lab and other classrooms. My own living quarters was a single room on the second floor, which doubled as the compound guest room when we had out-of-town visitors. My diet and daily lifestyle was Afghan as well, sleeping on the floor, eating without utensils from common serving dishes, a "squatty-potty" instead of raised toilets in the latrines.

I'd also become quite Afghan myself, at least on the outside. My beard was long. I wore the local *shalwar kameez,* a comfortable pajama-style drawstring pants covered by a long tunic, topped if weather dictated by a padded jacket and draped shawl, along with the typical flat, woolen hat called a *pakul*. And since green eyes like mine aren't so unusual among some Afghan ethnic groups, with my cultural and language skills I was often mistaken as a local.

In my daily life, becoming as much as possible like those around me was a benefit. For the sake of the Gospel, the Bible encourages God's servants to be all things to all people in order to win them to Christ (1 Corinthians 9:19-23). Still, urbanized single female expatriates surrounded by Kabul's cosmopolitan elite, foreign embassy delegations, and the growing male international community might not be too impressed with a bearded mountain man who would look right at home on America's TV Series, *Duck Dynasty*.

Although wearing local dress and having a beard was honorable and acceptable among Afghans, being a single man wasn't, especially one over thirty years old. When asked directly about my single state, I'd often joke, "Well, as you know, Jesus Christ was around my age, and He wasn't married either."

"Yes, we know, but you aren't Jesus!" I was told bluntly.

I did pray that if God was calling me to spend my life serving Afghans, He would provide me with a partner who shared this passion. But I didn't spend my days obsessing over finding a wife, probably because I was too busy. Still, by the summer of 2004 I was wrestling with my singleness enough to wonder if I should go back to the U.S. and base my ministry there, since it seemed a miracle would be needed to find a suitable helpmate in such a remote place.

My colleagues were aware of my struggle. One expat male friend, married with children, who was stationed in Feyzabad with another aid organization, approached me one day to ask, "So John, where are you at with this marriage thing? How are you really doing with being single?"

The question sent me to a room I used as my go-to retreat when I needed quiet time alone. There I cried out to God for His help and direction. I was wrestling with my loneliness and discouragement when I heard God's voice clearly.

To augment our regular team prayer times and weekly house church, I had collected some sermons and praise music. The message God was bringing to my mind was entitled *Doing Missions When Dying is Gain* by John Piper.

I located the cassette tape. It had been a long time since I'd listened to this particular sermon. The thrust of the message was dying to self in order to serve God. The Lord Jesus calls us to lay down our own desires as a daily living sacrifice just as He had laid down His own life for us on the cross.

By the end of the message, my heart was broken and my eyes wet. The choice before me was clear. Was I willing to lay down my own self and will on the altar to live and die in Afghanistan, trusting God with my future even if His choice for me was to remain single the rest of my life?

I've told the story of my crisis of faith in the book *A Flame on the Front Line*, so I won't repeat all the details here. Suffice it to say that the Lord prevailed and I came through it with a renewed commitment to stay the course in the land of my calling. It was a watershed moment of complete surrender and rededication to the Lord. I no longer had any doubt that God had a divine purpose for me to serve here in Afghanistan for such a time as this, whether single or married.

Bowing down in humble submission, I committed my life, hopes, vision, and singleness into the loving hands of my Heavenly Father. As I did so, I couldn't have imagined that the miracle I'd been longing for was only a phone call away.

5: JEANNE

AFTER A STINT TRAVELING back and forth to New York City to consult with clients, I moved there to work fulltime in 2000. I immediately began researching churches, especially those that offered opportunities to serve others in the community and abroad. Among those that interested me was Times Square Church (TSC), an interdenominational church with a weekly attendance of over seven thousand. TSC included around one hundred nationalities and met in a historic theater on Broadway just a few blocks from Times Square and Central Park.

Walking in for the first time, I sought out TSC's visitor information table and asked, "What ministries do you have in which someone like me could get involved?"

To me, the ministries in and through a local church, both locally and globally, were a good indication of its real heartbeat. I was impressed when the person staffing the table handed me a list of over thirty ministries. I was even more astonished to discover that TSC's founder and pastor was David Wilkerson, author of *The Cross and the Switchblade*, who had also helped start the Walter Hoving Home, the Bible-based substance abuse recovery program whose testimonies had impacted my adolescent heart while we lived in Italy.

TSC had three different Sunday worship services, each with a fresh message from God's Word. There was also a Tuesday evening service, Thursday night prayer meeting, and Friday night School of the Bible. I began attending every service I could, enjoying the presence of God, soaking in the teaching of God's Word, singing God's praises with all my heart, and passionately praying the promises of God.

Slowly, I was also becoming more and more discontented with my profession. I loved the work I was doing, but not the long hours, travel, stress, and pressure of multi-million-dollar projects. In consulting, you have to keep climbing up the corporate ladder or bail out. It's not uncommon to be working 24/7 on an urgent contract or even juggling responsibilities for various projects around the country. Since the job permitted no time for personal life, it was just as well that my few dating relationships had fizzled.

Nor did such a hectic schedule allow much time to serve God in the way I envisioned. I began feeling more and more compelled by the Holy Spirit that God was calling me to full-time service. In early 2001, I used my vacation time to participate in a short-term trip to help at an orphanage in Kosovo. This only whetted my appetite for overseas service.

After such an impactful trip, I began praying, "God, You know I love my profession, so You are going to have to give me a real dissatisfaction if You want me to leave it. Show me what You want me to do. Make it clear You are giving me Your go-ahead to quit my job."

But the gentle response I kept hearing from God was "not yet." During this time at TSC, Pastor David Wilkerson began preaching a message God was laying on his heart: "Hard times are coming for New York City. We must be ready. We must know God's Word! We need to watch and pray."

Sometimes Pastor Dave would break down weeping during his sermon because his heart was so burdened for New York City. We would sit in silence, praying quietly for NYC, until he could go on. Often, he'd ask, "Who has a read Bible?"

When people held up Bibles with red covers or red letters, he'd correct, "No, who has a Bible they've *read* and are reading daily?" Then he'd exhort further, "We must be in God's Word every day. Don't skimp! Study the Bible. Commit it to memory."

I myself was reading God's Word and praying, "Lord God, speak to me! Where do You want me to go? When can I resign from my job? I know You are calling me to serve You overseas, but I can't just give a two-week notice."

As I continued praying for direction, longing to hear God's voice, He gave me a picture of a map in my mind. I could see Central Asia, including Afghanistan, Pakistan, India, Nepal, and Tibet. *You are going there*, God spoke to me silently. I still didn't know the exact spot, but I knew the general region, and that was enough.

At last, I sensed God's peace and permission to leave my high-salaried consulting job. I put in a three-month notice and let my landlord know I wouldn't be renewing my lease. By this time, God was narrowing my focus of interest with one country after another falling off until only Afghanistan and Pakistan remained, then just

Afghanistan. I'd never had any prior interest in working in an Islamic country. And I knew little about Afghanistan except that I'd been born there.

Okay, God, I prayed. *I've always wanted to go back and see the country where I was born. If this is where You want me, I'll go.*

I had no idea how I'd get to Afghanistan or what I might do there. This was now early September 2001. I was just beginning to work off my three-month's notice and had driven to a client's site in Connecticut when I heard of the attack on the World Trade Center (WTC), just a few miles from my apartment. I had consulting projects at the WTC and friends who worked there. I'd like to think that if I had been actually working in NYC on 9/11, I would have headed straight to the WTC to volunteer my help.

As it was, it took five days before I was able to return to my apartment. The stench was terrible. Dust and soot hung in a filthy, black cloud over the city. I eventually found out that two of my friends had been among those who died when the towers collapsed.

No one in the TSC community had any doubt this was related to the disaster Pastor Dave had sensed coming. From weeping and prayer, the pastoral staff and congregation sprang to action. Feeding programs, grief counseling, clean-up, and other volunteer outreach were opened on site, and we'd often see firemen in full gear walking in from Ground Zero for a meal or cold drink.

In December, I'd finished working off my job notice and had moved out of my apartment. I was actually staying in a hotel, living off the hotel points I'd accumulated over years of travel. I was also volunteering at TSC wherever I could, including training for grief counseling for 9/11 survivors. I still had no idea what God had for me long-term. But one day I gathered up sufficient boldness to walk into the office of the church's missions director.

"I've resigned my job to serve wherever God wants me," I said. "I believe it might be in Afghanistan, but the Lord hasn't revealed the way yet. Is there anything you need done here at TSC that I could volunteer for?"

I gave a little background of my job experience, including internet and IT consulting. The missions director was a woman a few years older than me named Sue. She would become a close friend and mentor over the coming years, but at that moment she looked at me as though some escaped lunatic had wandered into her office.

"You know, people like you usually make me nervous," she said at last. "On the other hand, there actually is a need you might help with. You know we have a radio ministry here that broadcasts Pastor Dave's sermons in other languages. We need a website where listeners could go for discipleship and follow-up information."

I was delighted at the proposal. This was something I could definitely do, and I still had enough hotel points and savings to be able to offer my services for free. I loved working with the various translators from different countries.

By the time the project was nearing completion, a position opened in the church's missions department for coordinating short-term trips and ministry projects. I joyously accepted the position and soon found myself organizing itineraries, tickets, supplies, and other travel arrangements for short-term teams flying all over the world. I enjoyed both the challenge and working directly under Sue's tutelage.

But I was still thinking of Afghanistan, knowing that God had called me there. Every day I was praying and wondering when the door would open. While most Americans and other expats evacuated after 9/11, by this time many NGOs (non-governmental organizations) had returned along with new organizations starting humanitarian work there for the first time. With Sue's blessing, I began calling various NGOs, asking if they had any openings for Afghanistan. My initial thought was a three-month volunteer program.

I was willing to do anything needed. However, I did have a few specifications of my own. I wanted to work with an organization that shared my faith and values. Intercession is also one of my spiritual passions. One of the blessings of being able to leave behind my high-pressure consulting career was having time to rise early to spend hours with God, praying, worshipping, and reading the Bible before starting my day at TSC.

"Lord, I don't want to lose this," I pleaded. "Please help me find a place where I can serve you but still have time for prayer."

For months, God's answer seemed to be leaving me right where I was. Every organization I contacted informed me they had no current openings in Afghanistan. Their responses added up to the same skeptical query: "Are you sure you want to come at this time? Things are still quite a mess right now!"

Finally in early 2003, I received notice that one organization had an opening for an Information Technology (IT) specialist in Kabul. I knew immediately this was God's green light. Not only was the position a job I was uniquely qualified to fill, but the NGO's foundational principle and philosophy of ministry centered on intercessory prayer. Every morning from 8-10 a.m., the team met to read God's Word, sing praise songs, and pray before engaging in daily office or project work.

The only concern was that they requested a minimum two-year commitment. But I had absolute peace this was God's calling. So I agreed without hesitation.

In April 2003, I was still raising financial support when I was asked to lead a two-week medical aid trip to Kabul. I was hesitant at first since this was a highly experienced medical team and I knew nothing about medical work or pharmaceuticals. But our ministry director insisted I was qualified. Once I agreed, I found that my years in management consulting and the past months organizing travel itineraries and supplies were precisely the skills needed. In fact, it proved an excellent training experience for working as a single female in a male-dominated culture like Afghanistan.

My first visit to the land of my birth since I was three months old impacted me far more than I'd anticipated. We were holding a medical clinic in a village north of Kabul that had been devastated by the Taliban. During the fighting, the land had been mostly looted, the men and boys slaughtered, leaving the women and children to starve.

The area had once been a region filled with vineyards, which produced tons of grapes to eat and export. Sadly, the vineyards had been destroyed, leaving the villagers without a livelihood. To exacerbate the situation, refugees driven out by the Taliban were now filtering back from refugee camps in Pakistan, often with no more than the clothes on their backs, only to find their old homes burned or demolished.

My heart broke for the despair and pain I saw. God also filled me with a deep love for these hurting people. By the end of the trip, I knew God wasn't just calling me back to my birthplace for a short volunteer stint but to serve the Afghan people long-term. Ten weeks later in July 2003, I returned to Kabul to start my full-time humanitarian position.

Stepping off the plane, tucking my hair under a scarf, breathing in the hot, dusty air mixed with diesel fumes that is Kabul's unique fragrance, I knew I was home.

6: JOHN

IN THE SUMMER OF 2004, I accepted an invitation to participate in a training conference for international aid workers serving throughout Central Asia. During the Taliban era, I would have crossed the river and traveled overland to Dushanbe, capital of Tajikistan and home of our regional headquarters, to catch connecting flights. When I learned there was now a direct flight from Kabul to Istanbul, I made arrangements to fly from Feyzabad to Kabul. My plan was simple: make a brief stopover in Kabul to visit our NGO's central office, stay the night at a nearby guesthouse, see a friend in the morning, then fly on to Istanbul.

Once I deplaned, I hailed a taxi. Inching past a mounted Soviet MiG fighter jet marking the airport entrance, we headed down Airport Road into the city. After the calm of Feyzabad, Kabul felt like a madhouse. White Toyota Corolla hatchbacks, wood-framed *jinga* trucks, motorcycles, mule carts, and street vendors jostled late-model SUVs bearing acronyms of various governmental and aid organizations. All made way for the Hummers, Land Cruisers, and armored vehicles of the International Security Assistance Force (ISAF) convoys.

We eventually reached the NGO office on the opposite side of Kabul. I was relaxing in the foyer, drinking tea with a young engineer from the Panjshir who'd worked on projects with me in the north. Suddenly a vision of beauty walked through the front door.

Well, it was actually two women dressed modestly with head scarves, long-sleeved tops and long skirts. They took their shoes off at the door and appeared to be speaking Dari as they entered an office room. I assumed they were Afghan. But they were not wearing burqas. I'd been in a more conservative area long enough that I was a little shocked as well as intrigued to see uncovered female faces.

Straightening in curiosity, I asked my Afghan companion, "Do you know those two women who just came into the office? Do they work here?"

My companion looked surprised. "One is Afghan. The other is American like you. Don't you know her?" Like many locals, he assumed all Americans in Afghanistan were acquainted!

Now I was truly interested. The young woman my companion had indicated to be American was tall, slim, with her head scarf revealing just a hint of dark hair. As to her face, I couldn't have said what color her eyes were or exactly what she looked like, only that she was captivating. More significantly, here was a young lady who wasn't in Afghanistan on vacation but actually lived here. She spoke Dari and looked as Afghan as the young woman beside her.

As the two women returned to the foyer area, the Afghan woman showed recognition of my companion, greeting him respectfully. I found out later that she had once worked in the office. As I was introduced, I learned that her name was Tina while her American companion was Jeanne.

Since the post-9/11 media blitz and the release of *Inside Afghanistan,* much of the aid community knew who I was even if we'd never met in person. I could see from Jeanne's expression that she recognized my name. We spent a moment interacting. In Feyzabad, it would have been considered improper for me to be standing there conversing with women, but at a Kabul NGO office, international protocol applied.

Tina soon excused herself to see an expat friend in another office room. I remained chatting with Jeanne—but my mental wheels were racing. She certainly knew far more about me than I did about her. Casually, she mentioned, "You know, we have a mutual friend here in Kabul. Do you remember Ryan?"

Of course, I knew Ryan, an American in his mid-twenties who'd come to Feyzabad recently to work with me on a project.

"We've heard good things about the trip," Jeanne continued. "We were praying for him and your ministry and projects before he went."

By this point, I was becoming more and more intrigued with this incredible woman. Not only was she attractive, adapted to Afghan culture, and able to communicate in Dari, but she was also a spiritual person of faith and prayer. I quickly thought of a way to prolong our conversation.

"I'd love to contact Ryan while I'm here," I said. "Do you know how I might get in touch with him?"

"Yes, I do. Even better, I know where he lives. It's not far from here, but Kabul doesn't have street addresses. So how about if I take you in a taxi, then head home from there? It's no trouble at all. Just give me a moment to make my goodbyes."

Again the differences between Kabul and Feyzabad were evident. A woman would never be getting into a taxi alone with a male driver, much less with a male stranger, in my mountain home. Since I was delighted to spend more time with this charming new acquaintance, I offered no more protest as we headed out to the street to find a taxi. I ushered Jeanne into the back seat, then slid into the front by the driver since, as neither her husband nor family member, it wouldn't have been proper for me to sit next to her.

I lifted my hands to give thanks to God while exchanging the appropriate greetings with the taxi driver. Then I swiveled around to engage Jeanne in conversation. I was fascinated to discover that Jeanne had been born in Kabul, had a degree in IT (Information Technology), and a heart to serve Afghans. I also learned quickly that we had many mutual friends among the expat community.

When we reached the compound where Ryan lived, I didn't want this moment to end. Here was a rare gem that belonged in Afghanistan both by birth and calling. I longed to learn more about her. But I was now out of time. Even worse, once I flew to Istanbul, I wouldn't be returning to Feyzabad through Kabul, so I wasn't likely to ever see her again.

Ryan's living situation wasn't dissimilar to my own. The compound had a main house at the back where another expat family lived, then rooms along the wall that made up the small apartment where Ryan lived. Like most walled compounds, there was also a *chowkidar*, a combination unarmed guard and handyman. But when we knocked at the gate, it was the expatriate lady of the house who opened it. We stepped into the courtyard, where Jeanne introduced me.

Our hostess explained that Ryan wasn't home yet but would be returning shortly from their NGO office. Since the chowkidar had gone to the market, it wouldn't have been appropriate for Jeanne to leave me there alone, so the three of us chatted until Ryan showed up. He was almost a decade younger than me, extroverted and enthusiastic. Although I'd been enjoying my visit with Jeanne, it was good to see Ryan again as well.

We visited together until twilight began to darken the sky overhead. Ryan suddenly straightened up to exclaim, "Hey, John, it's getting late. Jeanne needs to get home before dark, and there's no taxi service around here. We need to get her to a main road where she can catch a taxi to the other side of the city."

I was still in a bit of culture shock over the idea of allowing a young lady to take a taxi alone. But I got to my feet and joined in the quick goodbyes, wondering what Ryan had in mind. Were we to walk Jeanne out to a major avenue?

I soon found out when Ryan wheeled out two bicycles. "There's no time to walk, so we'll take the bikes. This one is mine, and here is Michael's." Michael was our hostess's husband who was at an NGO meeting. Unlike Ryan's, the bike he was pushing in my direction had a good-sized luggage rack on the back. Ryan nodded towards it. "Jeanne will have to ride with you since my bike doesn't have a rack on the back."

I swallowed hard as I accepted the bike. The bikes themselves weren't a surprise. In a country where only the wealthy owned vehicles and even a motorcycle was a mark of prosperity, bicycles were a common family transport. I'd seen men pedaling along with their wife seated sidesaddle on a luggage rack behind him, a child or groceries on her lap. The problem was that I hadn't ridden a bike in years, much less with a passenger on the back and in Kabul's madhouse traffic.

I wasn't about to admit my nervousness in front of Jeanne. In my mind, I was anxiously praying. *Oh, Father, thank You for the opportunity to meet this godly lady who is now trusting me to drive her on this bike without crashing. Help me to do this without making a fool of myself!*

My emotions were bubbling over with exhilaration. Here was an eligible woman—exactly the type I would want to marry—beautiful, virtuous, sent here by God to serve, adapted to local culture and language, and who obviously loved Afghans. *Wow,* I may even have been thinking at this point, *Jeanne isn't just the type of woman but the very one I want to marry!*

That would entail not getting her killed on this bicycle before I ever got to know her. Fortunately, the first few streets were fairly empty, and I managed to stay upright as I peddled after Ryan. Relaxing slightly, I didn't even notice when my silent prayers became audible. I was no longer praying to stay upright, but passionately praying for Afghanistan, specifically for the people who lived on these streets, as I did everywhere I went.

When I realized I was praying aloud, I paused. To my surprise, my cycling companion spontaneously continued the prayer. It was a surreal experience to be pedaling after Ryan in increasing pedestrian and vehicle traffic while praying with the most wonderful woman I'd ever met in such a natural manner as if we might have been lifelong friends.

It wasn't long before we reached Darulaman Road. This was one of Kabul's main thoroughfares that dead-ended at the historic ruins of Darulaman Palace and included along its length hospitals, universities, government offices, and NGO headquarters, as well as the nearby Kabul Zoo and National Museum. Ryan's lodging was in the southern part of Kabul, where many international organizations had maintained headquarters and guesthouses long before the Russians, Taliban, or 9/11. Jeanne lived in northern Kabul, not far from the airport. To head north, Jeanne would have to cross the congested four-lane thoroughfare and flag down a taxi on the far side.

I didn't help Jeanne off the bike. Even a casual touch would be considered inappropriate on a public Kabul street. Once she slid to her feet, I dismounted as well. Ryan simply nodded to Jeanne as she prepared to cross the busy avenue. "Good to see you, Jeanne. God bless and take care of yourself."

I was aghast. Not even in America, much less in Afghanistan, would I leave a young lady to cross a busy thoroughfare to hail a taxi on her own, especially this late in the afternoon. Leaving my borrowed bike with Ryan, I caught up to Jeanne and walked beside her across the four lanes of traffic. Along the way, I asked Jeanne what the normal taxi fare was back to her neighborhood.

Once we reached the other side, I flagged down a taxi. As Jeanne entered the back seat, I took care of the fare and told the driver where she was going. After bidding her a brief farewell, I looked directly into the Afghan driver's eyes and instructed him to deliver her safely to her destination. Then the taxi pulled away.

I was already feeling separation anxiety like some lost puppy as the vehicle disappeared into the stream of traffic. I crossed back over to Ryan in a daze, barely avoiding collision with honking vehicles. I'd just met the woman of my dreams. What were the odds I'd ever again encounter such a perfect catch, someone with similar calling, interests, and passion to serve God right here inside Afghanistan?

Yet now she was gone—and I might never see her again. Especially since I'd be returning to Feyzabad from Istanbul through Tajikistan and would have no reason to revisit Kabul in the foreseeable future. I hadn't even thought to ask for her email or phone number.

In any case, even if we did meet again, why would such a remarkable lady, who'd recently worked in NYC and now in Kabul, be interested in a country boy like me?

7: JEANNE

AS I WALKED INTO THAT NGO office with my Afghan friend Tina, I didn't pay much attention to the two men sitting in the foyer. Yet I knew *about* John Weaver before ever arriving in Afghanistan, a story in its own right.

When I'd moved long-term to Kabul in July 2003, I lived with two other single expat women in a house within walking distance from our office. Initially, my job involved accounting and finances because of my background in mathematics. But since I had expertise in Information Technology (IT), I was also asked to do anything related to computer and internet needs. In addition, I studied Dari, the most common language spoken throughout Afghanistan.

Not all words or sounds translate well into other languages. That proved the case with my name, Jeanne. Thankfully, our Afghan NGO staff bestowed on me a beautiful local female name, Najiba, which means *distinguished, excellent, intelligent, or of noble birth.*

I loved my new name. It served as a reminder that I am indeed excellent and distinguished by noble birth as a member of God's royal family, daughter of the King of kings. A term of endearment, *jaan*, like *dear* in English, was routinely tacked onto the end of a name as indication of affection. So I was often called *Najiba-jaan.*

Working in such a multinational environment was a joyous return to my nomadic childhood years. My colleagues included German, Swiss, Argentinian, Dutch, Australian, British, Iranian, Brazilian, Romanian, Pakistani, Tajik, Afghan, as well as a few other Americans. The weekly expatriate worship gathering, which was Kabul's version of an international church service, encompassed more than fifty nationalities. Praying and worshipping God together with fellow followers of Christ from all over the world was a foretaste of heaven.

This was an environment tailor-made for a Kabul-born Foreign Service kid like me. With each passing month, I found myself falling more and more in love with Afghanistan and its people. The prompting of the Holy Spirit more than two years earlier had now deepened into a conviction that this place of my birth was to be part of my heart, soul, and mind for the rest of my life.

Yet it wasn't just Afghanistan with whom I yearned to fall in love. I was now thirty-two years old. I looked young for my age, especially since many Afghan women my age were often grandmothers already, aged by hard living and continuous childbearing. Since I didn't volunteer personal information, most Afghans assumed I was in my early twenties. Still, it was uncommon in Afghan culture for a woman of either age to be unwed.

When asked why I was still single, I gave an answer that was both truthful and acceptable in this culture of arranged marriages: "My father hasn't yet given permission for a man to become my husband."

If asked whether I'd be willing to marry an Afghan, I'd respond, "If God brought the right person and my parents approved. Of course, he must be a follower of Isa al-Masih since I'm a Christ-follower."

On this my interrogators could agree, which usually ended the discussion. For my part, my dreams of the future certainly included a husband and children. I'd had some dating relationships over the years, but these only made me tired of the rollercoaster emotional ups and downs of the American dating game. Once I'd fully committed my life to serving God, I became even more concerned that searching for Mr. Right would sidetrack me from a relationship with my Heavenly Father that was becoming more and more precious to me.

"Oh, God, I want my focus to be You," I prayed fervently, "not pursuing relationships that turn my life upside-down and end up going nowhere. So my prayer, Father God, is that You'll place a bubble around me that will protect me from emotional entanglement until You bring into my life the man You've chosen to be my husband."

That is exactly what happened. In fact, from that prayer forward, I'd felt no interest in the opposite gender except on one occasion. Knowing of my calling to Afghanistan, my immediate supervisor, Sue, had given me a recently-published book by an aid worker who'd been on the news during the U.S. invasion in October 2001. On the cover just above the title, *Inside Afghanistan,* was a photo of a man about my own age in Afghan clothing with a round, woolen *pakul* cap atop dark, curly hair and the most intense green gaze I'd ever seen.

As I picked up the book for a closer look, I heard the internal whisper I had come to recognize as the Holy

Spirit speaking to me: *This is your husband!* I was so startled I gave a gasp and dropped the book. When I picked it up, it was to tuck the book somewhere out of sight and mind. I wondered if I was just imagining things. But when the time came for my own crisis of doubt over marrying a virtual stranger named John Weaver, the Holy Spirit would calm my heart by gently reminding me of this experience.

By June 2004, I'd put the experience behind me to the point that I'd forgotten all about it. Coming up on the anniversary of my arrival in Afghanistan, I felt acclimatized enough that when a young American couple, Dustin and Amy, joined our team in Kabul, I took on the responsibility of helping them through cultural orientation. Through our larger Friday worship gatherings, we also included another American, Ryan, into our circle.

The four of us became close friends and formed a natural group for expat social activities. Not that Ryan and I were dating in any way. Ryan had become like a surrogate younger brother—and I considered him just that in the family of God.

By now I'd become fairly functional in Dari. Like many expat workers, I'd also adapted to wearing local Afghan clothes. This involved long skirts and loose-fitting, long-sleeved blouses or the female version of *shalwar kameez*, which were fashionably-embroidered tunics, always with pants underneath, since wearing a skirt, dress, or tunic in this culture without pants underneath would be as scandalous as forgetting one's underwear.

To top it off, I wore the long scarf that enveloped upper body as well as hair. I knew I was successfully assimilating when both Afghans and expat newcomers began mistaking me for a local—at least until I opened my mouth. My birthplace had become my home.

One thing that facilitated my cultural adaptation was spending time with Afghan friends. My closest friend, Tina, had been one of my language instructors. University-educated and cosmopolitan, she was far from typical in a country where most women remained illiterate. Her family was also part of Kabul's professional *intelligentsia* that had fled the country during the Taliban regime.

While in exile, she had become a follower of Isa al-Masih. Now that her family was back in Afghanistan, they'd decided it was time to arrange her marriage. In consideration of her faith in Christ, her parents had chosen an Afghan living in Germany, assuming he'd be less conservative and more understanding of his wife's beliefs than a local bridegroom.

Tina invited me to her engagement party. It was a cheerful gathering of women at her parent's house with the usual Afghan food, music, and dancing. Since few Afghan brides met their bridegrooms before the engagement and often even the wedding itself, Tina seemed content with her parents' choice.

But not long after the engagement party, I received a call from Tina. She asked me and our team to fast and pray for her. Her fiancé had arrived in Kabul. Only then had she discovered that he already had a wife in Germany and had no intention of taking her with him after the wedding. Instead, she'd be left at his mother's house in Kabul as a servant to help support his family. He had even tried to force her to consummate their impending nuptials. Devastated, Tina begged her parents to break the engagement.

"That is impossible," they told her. "He has already paid the dowry and provided bridal gifts. You have to go through with the marriage."

As requested, we interceded and fasted on Tina's behalf. God miraculously answered our prayers. Tina called to tell me the news with far more joy than when she had told me of her engagement. Though it meant substantial financial loss on their part, Tina's parents had conceded to her request, cancelling the wedding and returning the dowry. The bridegroom was so furious that Tina had to move around for fear his family might kidnap her to enforce the contract. But this didn't dampen Tina's spirits.

"I'm free! Praise God, I'm free!" she exulted on the phone. "Come and celebrate with me!"

I agreed to join her. Together we made the rounds of Tina's friends. We sat with each for tea, girl talk, and thanksgiving to God.

Tina had worked on various humanitarian projects and was also a language instructor, so several of our stops were at international aid organizations. The last place was clear across the city from my own house, a NGO where she had been employed for a short time.

I gave no thought to the two men sitting in the foyer as Tina and I entered an office room of female staff. We visited and drank tea while she gave her good news. After a time of sharing, Tina said, "Let's go see Tanya."

Tanya was one of the NGO's expat staff, a friend as well as former colleague of Tina when she worked there. As we walked out through the foyer toward Tanya's office, Tina recognized another former colleague, an Afghan engineer, who was sitting with a man in Western clothing. As soon as I was introduced, I recognized John's name and not just from the cover graphic of *Inside Afghanistan*. My friend Ryan had recently visited Feyzabad and came back raving about the fabulous work John Weaver and his team was doing there.

Unlike the picture on his book cover, John wasn't wearing Afghan dress. I learned later that this was because he was flying to an international conference. I can admit to feeling intrigued and even rather star-struck to meet a man I'd heard so much about and to discover he was as handsome and charming in person as on a television screen.

Tina soon excused herself politely to talk with Tanya. By now, the Afghan engineer had left as well, leaving me chatting with John Weaver. He proved an easy conversationalist. We exchanged the usual background chitchat of two Americans serving abroad. I discovered John was born in Virginia, not far from where my parents lived, and that his parents now lived in North Carolina near where I had attended university.

I found myself thoroughly enjoying our discussion. I was even a bit disappointed when John mentioned he was just flying through to Istanbul and would return back to the north via Tajikistan. So when he asked how he might get in contact with our mutual acquaintance, Ryan, I was more than happy to extend our dialogue by showing John the way to Ryan's home.

As Tina and Tanya returned to the foyer, I told them about the plan to accompany John to Ryan's house. Since this was Tina's last stop, she'd already arranged a ride home. So both Tina and Tanya assured me that it was fine to go with John.

When we arrived at Ryan's via taxi, only the wife of the Swiss family that shared the compound was home. It would have been inappropriate to leave John there alone with her, so it was only good manners to wait until Ryan arrived, right?

And once Ryan arrived, I made no effort to leave either. We were having so much fun I was startled to notice the late hour. Kabul in 2004 was peaceful compared to earlier or even later years, but for a woman to travel alone after dark was still unwise and even dangerous.

I felt a little awkward when Ryan arranged for John to transport me on the back of our host's bike. At the same time, I was ecstatic. I'd seen women zipping around Kabul on the back of bikes and always wanted to try it. A few times, I'd even voiced my wish to God. I call these my "half-prayers." Not really asking anything from God, just sharing a desire.

Psalm 37:4 tells us, "Delight yourself in the LORD, and He shall give you the desires of your heart." Time and time again, I've seen my Heavenly Father answer not just deep-heart prayers, but even simple wishes like a bike ride, just as loving earthly parents often grant a child's wish simply to put a smile on his/her face.

This was one of those times. The bike ride was as adventurous and thrilling as I'd imagined. Especially with this man who in such a short time had captured my attention and maybe even my heart.

Then John began to pray. With thanksgiving, he prayed for our bike trip and that I'd find a taxi and be taken safely home. He also prayed for the walled houses we wheeled by, for the people behind those walls needing God's saving grace, for the needs of this turbulent, war-torn country in which we were living.

When he paused, my own prayers welled up to fill the silence. Only long afterwards did I learn that John was nervous as he competently steered us down bumpy, dusty streets and through traffic. What impressed me was the way he prayed, as though engaged in an intimate conversation. Not to mention the passion for God and the Afghan people I could hear in his tone.

Wow! Just who is this guy who prays as naturally as he breathes and who I in turn feel so at ease praying with?

But I had no more time to find out because we'd reached Darulaman Road, where I was to catch my taxi. My heart was moved again when John insisted on crossing the busy thoroughfare with me and meeting the taxi driver before permitting him to drive off with me. As the taxi merged into northbound traffic, John had already blended into the crowds. Would our paths ever cross again?

I found myself dreaming that the answer would be yes.

8: JOHN

I EVENTUALLY ARRIVED at the NGO guesthouse where I was booked to stay the night. This was Thursday evening, the weekend in Kabul since Friday was the Muslim equivalent to the Jewish Sabbath or Christian Sunday. One of the other expats staying at the guesthouse recognized me and asked, "John, would you be interested in going with me tomorrow to the Friday gathering?"

Yes I was interested. Not only to worship together with other believers, but also because I knew a friend would be there with whom I needed to discuss a project we were working on up in Badakhshan. Since I had to catch the flight to Turkey, I left the guesthouse in the morning prepared to head straight to the airport from the gathering.

Kabul's expat faith community met in one large group every other Friday and in smaller home groups scattered around the city the Friday in between. This was a small group weekend, and as we arrived at the designated house, I could hear an electronic keyboard, guitar, and voices singing a well-known worship chorus.

Stepping through the doorway, I saw thirty to forty men, women, and children seated on spread-out rugs and tushaks. At first glance, I realized I wasn't such a stranger here. Because of the international exposure created by the book *Inside Afghanistan,* my involvement in helping other NGOs get started after 9/11, as well as various collaborative humanitarian projects, I recognized a lot of people.

Yet only one registered. As I entered the room, it felt like the climax of some screen classic with time itself slowing down and the music rising to a crescendo. All eyes were on the song leader. My companion and I weren't making enough noise to draw attention. But as though some invisible thread connected us, I saw Jeanne's head turn my direction the moment I walked through the door, her gaze seeking out mine. The joyous smile that lit up her angelic face made my heart race.

Maybe she was just being welcoming to a newcomer. Nevertheless, when I saw an open spot on the tushak next to Jeanne, I chose to take her smile as an invitation. There was no opportunity to speak. We exchanged nods as I settled beside her. For now, it was enough just to be singing and praising God side by side.

Then I saw the person I'd hope to meet. Since he too had to leave early, we'd made arrangements to slip out and chat briefly. We both made our way unobtrusively out into the courtyard. I dealt with our business as quickly as possible so as not to waste a single moment with Jeanne. Especially since a glance at my watch reminded me I'd need to leave soon if I was to reach the airport on time.

But when I stepped back into the meeting room, Jeanne wasn't there. In fact, the group was now much smaller. A glance around told me the children were also gone. It didn't take much to guess that Jeanne must be helping with children's church.

Crestfallen, I wandered back outside. Seeing Jeanne here this morning had been such an unexpected bonus that it felt anticlimactic to not even get to say goodbye. Maybe I could find the children's church, think up some excuse to interrupt long enough to make a proper farewell. After all, with as much noise as kids make, how hard could it be to track them down?

However, I couldn't hear a single sound that might be children. I didn't bother with the first floor since it was taken up by the main meeting room and washrooms. Spotting a staircase, I sprinted up the steps to the second floor. There was a row of doors. I listened at each to no avail. These kids were sure quiet!

I was feeling rather foolish by now. Yet I wasn't about to give up. With a soft knock, I began opening each door in turn. I hit a home run on the third door. I now saw why the children were so silent. They were listening to Jeanne teach a Bible story. She broke off when she saw me step into the room.

I'm an extrovert by nature and a communicator/teacher by spiritual gifting. So it is a rare moment that finds me at a loss for words. But as I stood there, the children's eyes now fixed on me, Jeanne's own expression questioning why I'd interrupted her class, my mouth went dry and my mind totally blank. Then Jeanne excused herself, turning the class over to a co-worker. Jeanne stepped out into the hall and closed the door between us and the class.

The delay gave me time to muster up some fumbling dialogue. "Jeanne, it was so nice to meet you. I'm leaving now for the airport. I just wanted to say goodbye and thank you for helping me get in contact with Ryan. The Lord bless you, Jeanne."

I wanted to steer the conversation to the subject of keeping in touch. But I lacked the courage or the clarity of what to say. Even more so because once I returned to Feyzabad, my only available phone service would be a sat-phone, which we kept for emergency use only since its usage fee was $1.50 a minute. This wasn't because Afghanistan had no cell-phone service. I'd witnessed Jeanne using one to call Ryan. But cell-towers were just being constructed in our remote mountain area.

Jeanne responded to my fumbling goodbyes matter-of-factly. "By the way, you left your Bible when you went out. I didn't know if you'd already left for the airport, so I gave it to so-and-so to get it back to you."

I knew the mutual acquaintance she mentioned and thanked her. I finally tore myself away, wishing there was more time to spend getting to know Jeanne. Though in truth I had no idea whether this lovely lady had the slightest interest in ever crossing paths with me again!

9: JEANNE

I'M NOT SURE WHAT TURNED my head just as John
stepped through the doorway. John's impact and
influence in the international aid community was
apparent by the excitement of others as he entered the
room. My own heart skipped a beat. It then accelerated
as he purposefully worked his way through the group to
sit down beside me. I'd already noticed that his smile lit
up his face all the way to his green eyes. And now those
eyes were smiling at me.

Okay, God, I reminded in a quick prayer, *I asked You
to keep me in a bubble until You bring into my life the man
You intend for my husband. I don't want to be feeling any
emotional entanglement here if You have no future plan in
this.*

Was John's sudden vanishing act God's answer?
Another expat colleague and I were on the roster that
morning to teach children's church. When John still
hadn't returned by the time we led the children upstairs,
I firmly tamped down my disappointment. After all, I
hadn't expected to see him again anyway. Still, it would
have been nice to say goodbye.

I'd resigned myself to not seeing him again. So I was
as surprised as I was happy when John burst into
children's church looking for me. Surely he wouldn't
have bothered if he didn't have some interest in me as I

did in him. But his farewells were dutiful, and he made no mention of wanting to stay in contact. Had I misread his interest?

Over the following weeks, I tried to put the experience out of my mind. It would be different if John Weaver lived in Kabul where God might keep bringing him across my path. But with John living on the far side of Afghanistan's northeastern mountain chain, there was little point in thinking about someone I might never see again.

Besides, hadn't I already determined I'd no interest in marrying an American? Having grown up in a multicultural context, I'd struggled with culture shock moving back to the U.S. Especially with what seemed an insular attitude of superiority and indifference by too many Americans towards the rest of the more than seven billion people on the planet.

My image of an American husband was a stereotype I'd seen too often perpetrated on TV—a balding, paunchy guy slouched in a recliner with a beer in one hand and a TV remote in the other, too glued to the sports channels to pay any attention to his wife and family or affect any meaningful change in this world.

Not that John Weaver appeared to be that type of American male, at least based on what I had seen during our short acquaintance. Still, since advancing that acquaintance seemed unlikely, I pushed any lingering thoughts of him from my mind.

It must have been two months later when my cell-phone rang as I was working at my desk. I didn't recognize the number, so I was tempted to just let it ring.

Then I realized it was an international number. Not wanting whoever was calling to be wasting their money on overseas rates, I snatched up the phone.

The deep male voice wasn't one I'd heard on the phone before nor expected to. "Hi, this is John Weaver. May I speak to Jeanne?"

10: JOHN

THE TRIP TO ISTANBUL proved a profitable experience, although on the flight home I was thinking more about Jeanne than my short summer excursion. I'd flown to Kabul having totally surrendered my will to remaining single if that were God's choice for me. Now God had brought across my path the epitome of the woman I had dreamed of marrying. Surely this couldn't be coincidence.

Maybe God was just testing my resolve to follow Him unreservedly. After all, this impressive woman might be living in Afghanistan, but Kabul with its electricity, running water, hospitals, supermarkets, larger expat community, and active social scene was a far cry from Feyzabad. Not to mention, Jeanne was one classy lady and I was a bearded hillbilly. We were literally mountains apart.

Several more days passed before I met my expat friend Kurt, who had asked me about marriage before my flight to Kabul. When he asked about my trip, I answered, "You won't believe this, but I met someone incredibly special in Kabul. I'm wrestling with whether or not I should pursue getting to know her."

Kurt had never met Jeanne, but he knew about her. He'd lived in Kabul before and knew many of Jeanne's previous and current team members, especially Georg, her NGO director. Kurt listened patiently to my enthusiastic ravings before counseling, "Well, I guess you need to commit the matter to prayer."

"I'm doing just that," I responded. "But I can't help thinking I've failed at this twice. And even though I never thought to meet a woman like her in Afghanistan, Kabul is a long way from Feyzabad. What if I take the risk of pursuing a relationship and she isn't willing to relocate to this area? Is it worth stirring up all the emotions involved, as well as the possible heartbreak, if God wants me to remain single?"

He had no answer. However, he did pray for me and promised to continue praying. Not in my wildest dreams could I have guessed that not so many months later Kurt would be pronouncing Jeanne and me husband and wife.

I continued to pour my energies back into my work, of which there was plenty. Beyond the immediate demands of disaster relief projects and longer-term community development programs, I was dealing with another crisis. For various security reasons, my current NGO would no longer be sponsoring me once my work visa expired in September 2004.

In hindsight it was a wise decision. Yet during the difficult transition, I was wondering, praying, and asking, "What is God doing?"

As September arrived, there was a new development that might hold the key to solving my visa dilemma. A German woman was scheduled for a short-term work visit. It was my responsibility to make arrangements to transport her from Kabul up to Feyzabad.

About this same time, my expat friend Kurt reminded me, "I've been praying for you. Have you had any further contact with Jeanne?" I'd had no contact with Jeanne except possibly in my daydreams. Even if she remembered our brief encounter, I had no valid reason to call her out of the blue.

Then it occurred to me I did have an excuse for using that expensive sat-phone. The NGO with which Jeanne worked had German expats who would be perfect for welcoming our German guest. Besides, Jeanne's country director, Georg, would be the best person to ask about a work visa. So I emailed our mutual friend Ryan and asked for Jeanne's cell-phone number, which he emailed back.

Okay, if it was only about logistics, it would have made more sense to just call her office. The real truth was that I just wanted to hear Jeanne's voice again. I waited impatiently as her number rang and rang. At last I heard her calm voice—such a sweet sound to my ear. Jeanne agreed unhesitatingly to pick up our German guest at the Kabul Airport. Georg was actually out of the country at the moment, but Jeanne would pass along my visa request.

The conversation was brief. By the end, I was no longer vacillating on how to get our German visitor from Kabul to Feyzabad. When was the next flight to the big city?

11: JEANNE

I PUT DOWN THE PHONE. Why had John Weaver called my cell phone instead of our NGO office or someone higher up in authority? Could I hope he just wanted to hear my voice as much as I wanted to hear his?

I was happy to help John's German volunteer. But I had no authority to promise him a visa letter. Georg was currently out of the country as were several other senior colleagues. I had no way to even contact Georg in the short window by which John needed his new visa.

Since I handled the accounting and other administration, Georg had left me his electronic signature in case important work orders or money transfers needed signed without delay. And I knew Georg well enough to know he'd give John a visa at the drop of a hat. So I drew up the official NGO work visa request letter.

What I forgot to do was tell Georg. Only several months later after he returned from his furlough did I remember to inform him. As I had anticipated, he was pleased to add John Weaver to our team.

Because I'd already made arrangements for picking up and hosting the German volunteer, I wasn't expecting John to walk into my office a week later to pick up his visa letter in person. Once again, we fell into easy conversation as though we'd known each other for years.

I had to remind myself, *Okay, this is just a casual interchange between two friendly acquaintances. After all, he's flying back to Feyzabad tomorrow, so the situation is no different than on our last encounter.*

But my heart wasn't listening to my mind. Somehow, I found myself offering to organize an outing to fill the hours John would be waiting for his guest's flight. I rounded up my American teammates, Dustin and Amy, as well as Ryan, so we'd be properly chaperoned. Amy and I packed a picnic lunch. Ryan brought along his guitar.

Dustin drove us out to Paghman, a garden district about thirty kilometers up into the mountains above Kabul. War had largely destroyed the lush public gardens Afghanistan's last king had built there, but there were still scenic orchards, vineyards, and streams. We spread out a bamboo mat, gave thanks to God, and enjoyed an Afghan lunch of *naan* bread, cheese, sliced cucumbers, and tomatoes.

We were all dressed in Afghan clothing. Amy and I followed local protocols of keeping our heads well-covered and the soles of our feet discreetly tucked out of sight. Otherwise we were just five young people enjoying each other's company. We prayed, sang songs to Ryan's strumming, and talked. Once again, I was struck at how natural it felt to be praying, singing, and talking with this John Weaver, though not once did our own personal interaction stray beyond the group dynamic.

I didn't allow myself to think of other factors like his rugged good looks, intense green eyes, and smile that lit up his face so irresistibly it was impossible not to respond. After all, we'd shortly be picking up the pieces of our picnic and driving back to Kabul. Then he'd be gone again—maybe permanently this time.

Resolutely, I pushed him from my mind. I was determined to focus instead on my upcoming trip back to the U.S. for the Christmas holidays. That bubble of mine was becoming increasingly fragile. If I weren't careful, it might pop!

12: JOHN

GRATEFUL TO HAVE THE visa letter finally in hand, I journeyed back to Feyzabad with our German visitor. At least the letter put off any concerns about leaving Afghanistan.

I'd also reveled in spending more time with Jeanne, so much that it had been hard to board my return flight. I couldn't have said what we'd talked about or eaten at that picnic. But I was left with an unforgettable impression of green beauty, serenity, and the joy of camaraderie with these new friends who weren't just fellow Americans but fellow siblings in God's family. And I could no longer deny that I was falling in love with one of them.

Yet I returned home as conflicted and unsure as before. My four picnic companions had an easy give-and-take that bespoke of close friendship, often speaking of people, events, and even belongings to which I was an outsider. At one point they were discussing some kind of water bottle they owned that sounded like "now-Jean", joking about the similarity to Jeanne's name. I had no idea what they were talking about. Eventually, I learned what a Nalgene water bottle was and even came to own one myself. But it was a reminder of the wide gap between Kabul and my simple life in Feyzabad.

I'd come full circle to my previous struggle. What elegant, intelligent lady would have any interest in coming to a place like Feyzabad or marrying a mountain man like me? Especially one who lived in the big city of Kabul where good-looking, interesting—and, yes, godly—single men were plentiful within the growing expat community. All of whom would be falling head over heels to court a pretty woman like Jeanne.

Still, I couldn't let myself dwell on such thoughts. Not just because they were dishonoring to the Lord to whom I'd committed my life, whether single or married, but because we had a lot of project work to complete before the winter snow arrived. While the roads remained clear, I traveled to the regional Ministry of Foreign Affairs (MFA) in Kunduz with the work visa letter Jeanne had given me in Kabul.

God paved the way because the local MFA director turned out to be an old acquaintance as well as a person of peace. He was a refugee in Tajikistan when I first met him, but he'd returned to Afghanistan after 9/11. We settled down to drink several cups of tea, a very important social ritual. Within the hour I had my new work visa.

I was now technically working for the same NGO as Jeanne, but I refused to let my feelings or thoughts wander in that direction. Especially since with my current work schedule and winter fast approaching, nothing short of a miracle would bring me across Jeanne's path again any time before spring.

13: JOHN

MAYBE IT WAS A MIRACLE—at least it seemed so to me. It started with a simple request to facilitate an Australian student who needed an internship in international aid to complete her college degree.

Esther was willing to do anything, but she could only come for two weeks in January. Feyzabad was her first choice because she'd read *Inside Afghanistan* and had the idea that John Weaver was some kind of Indiana Jones. Or more like a combination of Hudson Taylor and Jim Elliot, taking the good news of Christ's great love to people and places under the most extreme of conditions.

Because of the likelihood of being snowed-in this time of year, I was disinclined to give my consent. I also had objections because two weeks was hardly enough of an internship to accomplish anything. But the person who recommended Esther felt she had potential to be a long-term worker. And certainly anyone willing to travel alone into the rugged mountains of the Hindu Kush in the dead of winter had commitment. So I finally said yes.

For air travel, we relied on humanitarian aviation services such as ASI. Ranging from one-engine Cessna Continentals to Super King Airs that could carry a dozen passengers and five tons of cargo, ASI planes flew into conflict areas and war zones where commercial flights couldn't or wouldn't dare venture.

ASI had one or two flights a week into Feyzabad's single airstrip, depending on weather and availability. Some weeks there were no flights at all. In mid-January, despite a blizzard in Kabul, they managed to drop off our young Australian intern.

Esther was a delight to our entire community. And she definitely proved to be a diligent worker, learning some basic culture and language, helping homeschoolers with their studies, tutoring English, and conducting interviews with locals and expats to complete her program requirements.

All the while the weather continued to worsen. We'd built in a tiny window of leeway for bad weather in scheduling Esther's return to Kabul to catch her flight back to Australia. This proved providential because when the day of her departure came, so did a snowstorm. Due to weather and other commitments, ASI couldn't make up the cancelled flight. We'd have to wait for the next regularly scheduled one.

We were down to the wire. If the plane couldn't come as scheduled the next morning, the only hope for Esther to make her flight home would be to drive her overland to Kabul. But this wasn't as easy or straightforward as it sounded.

The first 200 kilometers of road from our remote, northeastern location was rugged unpaved dirt, mostly covered in snow by now. Then we'd have to cross over the Salang mountain pass at almost 3,500 meters or 13,000 feet elevation. The road through the mountains was narrow and twisting, jagged potholes making its occasional paved stretches almost worse than the dirt sections. It was also routinely cut off by avalanches in the winter.

But the road itself wasn't as infamous as its most dangerous segment, a tunnel 2.67 kilometers (1.66 miles) long at the height of the Salang pass. Built by the Russians back in the 1960s, it had been left to crumble away after the Soviet withdrawal and was so poorly ventilated that people trapped inside by avalanches or stalled traffic had died of carbon monoxide poisoning or frozen to death.

On the plus side, our Feyzabad office possessed a good truck and an even better driver. I myself rarely drove for several reasons. First, it is a high-risk occupation, whether inching over slippery mountain passes, avoiding landmines, evading bandits, or braving the lawless city traffic. Second, it is a good-paying profession in a place where the locals desperately need employment. So it made sense to give the job to someone more experienced than me rather than risk my own neck behind the wheel, not to mention the lives of others.

It was also a gesture of trust as it involved me as a foreigner entrusting my life and safety into the hands of an Afghan. Not just from a vehicle accident, but Taliban and other enemies who didn't care for westerners, especially Americans. Our local driver had become a good friend, indeed someone I'd trust to risk his life on my behalf. He was also one of the best drivers I'd ever known. So I respected his judgment on whether the truck could make the crossing in this weather.

The next morning came. Sure enough, we were informed it was snowing too hard for takeoff in Kabul.

The earliest they could reschedule would be the following week. I tried to check road conditions, but the reports were inconclusive. I left the decision to our Afghan driver.

"Sure, we can do it!" he said with absolute confidence. "When do you want to go?"

Our Australian intern Esther didn't mind the change of plans at all. She had an adventuresome streak a mile wide or she wouldn't have come to Feyzabad mid-winter. Having never seen snow before this trip, she was also having the time of her life with the white stuff and was thrilled at the prospect of crossing entire mountains covered with it.

As for me, I told myself that my willingness to personally escort Esther overland had nothing to do with a delightful lady who lived at our destination. After all, I had not so much as spoken to Jeanne since September. Over the past few months, I'd come to terms with my singleness. By now Jeanne was probably dating one of those nice guys working in Kabul.

No, I was taking this trip solely because it was my responsibility as Esther's supervisor to make sure she returned safely to Australia. None of which explained my sense of hope as our Afghan driver got the truck ready. Or why I made sure I had Jeanne's cell number on-hand.

The pass was as snow-packed and ice-cold as anticipated. This actually proved a blessing since deep, frozen ruts and high snowbanks kept our vehicle firmly away from the cliff edge. Precipices dropped sheer from the narrow, winding road to still-verdant river valleys hundreds of meters below. Clusters of mudbrick compounds and shepherd boys herding flocks of hardy mountain goats gave evidence humanity had penetrated even to this high elevation.

By late night, we'd arrived at a small town where some friends gave us lodging. We left again at first light, praying that the Salang Tunnel would be open when we reached it. Thankfully, we had no problems passing through the long, ice-filled passageway. By evening, we crested yet another ridge. Spread out below and creeping up hillsides could be seen the galaxy of flickering yellow and fluorescent-white lights that was Kabul at night.

Once we reached the guesthouse where I'd booked lodging, I found out that Esther's early morning flight was still a go. However, another blizzard headed for Kabul might cancel later flights. I didn't even pretend disappointment. On the contrary, it was all I could do to curb my own growing sense of anticipation. I had absolute confidence this surprising sojourn in Kabul was part of God's sovereign plan. Late though it was, I now had a good reason to call Jeanne.

Only then did it occur to me that I didn't even know if Jeanne was still in-country. After all, we hadn't communicated since last September. Still, if this trip was God's initiative to put us in face-to-face contact again, then God would also have orchestrated for her to be in Kabul.

"Hello? This is Jeanne."

My heart jumped when I heard the soft female voice answering the call. So she *was* in-country.

"Hi, Jeanne, this is John Weaver from Feyzabad. I'm in town rather unexpectedly." I briefly explained what had brought me to Kabul. "I wanted to touch base to check whether Georg is back in-country and if he's onboard with me being under his leadership and NGO umbrella. I wondered if I might stop by tomorrow after I get our guest boarded for her flight. Do you still have the morning prayer meeting?"

"Yes. 8 a.m. every morning."

"Would it be okay if I dropped by to join you? And chat with Georg about how this merger is going to work?"

"Absolutely! Georg isn't back yet, but I'm sure you can discuss things with our interim team leader." Her tone was warm, welcoming—dare I even hope a little eager? My sense of anticipation amplified to another level.

Suddenly it dawned on me that tomorrow was my birthday. I couldn't think of any better gift than the chance to see sweet Jeanne's smiling face again.

14: JEANNE

FIVE MONTHS. THAT'S HOW long it had been since I'd heard a single word from John Weaver. I had successfully managed to push him from my mind in part because I'd been so busy.

In December I'd flown to Moscow, where my parents were serving a Foreign Service assignment at the American Embassy, then on to the U.S for a few weeks. The trip had been an enjoyable tour of family, friends, and speaking at churches. I'd arrived back in Kabul the first week of February having reconciled myself not to see or hear from John again.

So I was not pleased that my heart skipped a beat when an unfamiliar number on my cell-phone turned out to be John Weaver. Once again he'd called my personal number. Was this just because he had my number most easily at hand?

John's stated reason for calling at this late hour was whether he could drop by the office the next morning. Did he just want to iron out the new collaboration of our partnership in the north? Or did he want to see me personally?

I had my heart under control again until John walked in the next morning. In his mountain garb—shalwar kameez, padded vest, and long, woolen scarf—he looked like some princely warrior, his green eyes even more intense than I remembered against darkly-tanned features, his tight, dark curls under the *pakul* cap longer than on our last encounter.

Our prayer time had already started when he entered, so we didn't speak. But his gaze went immediately to mine. I was so thrilled that I remember little of what we were praying for until someone announced that today was John's birthday.

15: JOHN

JOINING THE TEAM PRAYER meeting felt like coming home to family. The guesthouse was in a typical Kabul compound with a high perimeter wall, a courtyard with a grape trellis, and a two-story house at the back. I was running late by the time I put Esther on her flight, so I could already hear singing as the chowkidar opened the gate and escorted me indoors.

Despite that work visa Georg had granted, I was still an outsider to this group. But any such feeling immediately dissipated as I was pulled into their team time. I found I knew more of them than I'd expected. If Georg wasn't yet back from Germany, there was the young American couple from the picnic last fall along with others I'd encountered on various projects around the country.

But I had eyes for only one person. Since no opportunity had presented itself for personal conversation, I could only hope Jeanne was as happy to see me as I was to see her. Just being in her presence again, praying and lifting our voices in praise to God, filled my heart with joy and peace. Here I was in Jeanne's world. These were her people and team. Yet they were now embracing me with as much welcome as though I too was a part of this family.

I don't know who let it slip that it was my birthday. But someone announced, "We're so glad John could be with us today. Since it's his birthday, let's take some time to pray for him."

Before I knew it, I found myself seated in a chair while the others gathered around to pray for me. My heart swelled with emotion as one after another, including Jeanne, prayed God's blessing on my life, work, and future. I don't know if her teammates had any clue I might have a special interest in Jeanne or she in me. The American couple at least knew of our past contact. Certainly no one linked openly the names of John and Jeanne. However, when one of the married women prayed that God would bless my relationships, I heard it as a prophetic utterance and perhaps as confirmation of my pursuit of their wonderful teammate.

By the end of that prayer session, I felt adopted by the team as if I were an absent son returning home. I also felt an overwhelming sense of God's favor and blessing, of hope and optimism for my future. Maybe my Heavenly Father was up to something, and this beauty who had caught my eye was front and center of His plan.

I managed a private chat with Jeanne at the end of the meeting. Again, I cannot remember the content of that conversation, just the joy of being in her presence. I let her know I'd be in town a day or more, depending on when ASI scheduled a flight to Feyzabad. Could I see her later? Walk her home? Join the team prayer meeting tomorrow morning?

The rest of that day set a pattern for the week. I walked Jeanne home. We took a leisurely route so as to have more time for conversation. As before, we talked, laughed, and shared our hearts as though we'd been friends for years. We also prayed together as automatically and naturally as on our first acquaintance.

Snow fell that day and the next and the next. I didn't even consider trying to return to Feyzabad overland. Giving our local driver some travel funds, I told him, "Thank you again for driving us safely to Kabul. Here's money to use for food, lodging and fuel for the truck. Whenever you're ready, take the truck back to Feyzabad."

Around 6 a.m. each morning, I called ASI to check on flights. Each morning they responded, "Sorry, John, not today."

With no other place to go, I would then head over to the team prayer meeting. After that, Jeanne and I would make plans for the day. This was our first opportunity to interact freely with each other as single adults. Not that we were dating, per se, at least not in the unchaperoned, one-on-one sense that would be the norm back in the U.S. Such behavior would be inappropriate in Afghanistan. Jeanne and I had also committed to maintain a pure testimony of conduct that would be honoring to God and not offensive in any way to our Afghan colleagues.

But Kabul's expat scene was an active one. Every day we were invited to some social gathering or group outing. I was always at Jeanne's side. Without anything being said, our expat colleagues began treating us as though we were a couple. Several even said they were praying for our relationship.

I was now staying in the team guesthouse, just two streets over from the office. The compound where Jeanne lived with several other single female expats was also a few blocks away. This was a part of Kabul with many international organizations, embassies, and restaurants. At that time in 2005, the area was relatively safe. So Jeanne and I did a lot of walking, strolling at a leisurely pace from the office to her home, a restaurant, or a planned activity to stretch out those precious moments of togetherness and private conversation.

Each passing day only strengthened my attraction to this godly woman. I remember one day asking Jeanne a question as we were walking down the street. She didn't turn her head my way, but was saying softly, "Jesus! Jesus! Jesus!"

Then I realized she hadn't heard me. Focused on a nearby huddle of burqas and malnourished children, she was crying out in prayer her burdened distress for them. Again, I was incredibly impressed and moved by her compassion for the people of Afghanistan. We began making intentional prayer walks part of our daily routine.

When we couldn't bring ourselves to break off our conversation, we would head over to the guesthouse. The hostess, an older expat named Miss Irene, was delighted to play chaperone. Hurrying us into the living area, she'd direct, "You two sit right here and visit. I'll go make tea."

She'd then make sure we had some face-to-face time before bustling out with a tea tray. Throughout all this, the weather remained a winter wonderland. With no central heat and only the occasional gas space heater, we were always bundled up and chilled. Yet my memories of those days are of an enchanted, sun-drenched hiatus I wanted to go on forever.

But each day I was also aware this hiatus couldn't last. Sooner or later, the skies would open and I'd have no further excuse to stay in Kabul. Just as before, I could be gone at a moment's notice with no idea when I might return. I knew Jeanne must be wondering if I was ever going to verbalize my intentions.

In truth, I didn't know how to go about that in Afghanistan. The proper protocol would be to first get permission from her parents. Then her country director, team leader, or NGO boss would be consulted. But Georg wasn't yet back in-country. And if I did make my intentions known, how would we go about dating if I was in Feyzabad and Jeanne in Kabul? At least I'd finally acquired a cell-phone so we could call each other.

Valentine's Day fell exactly one week after my arrival. Bad weather was still grounding any flights. Jeanne and I made dinner plans to join other singles at an international restaurant known for its delicious steaks and musical karaoke.

In recognition of the holiday, I wrote Jeanne a little "Be My Valentine" note to express my feelings. I might have even included those significant words: "I love you." In Afghanistan, shoes aren't normally worn inside but left lined up outside the front door. Finding what I thought were Jeanne's shoes, I slipped the note into one of them.

That evening, I picked Jeanne up in a taxi. I wondered what she thought of my "valentine." But when she didn't bring it up, I didn't either. If she thought my gesture was a silly one, at least she was too polite to let me know. The rest of the evening was wonderful. We all tried our hand at karaoke. At some point, I used my new cell-phone to call my mom 8 ½ time zones earlier in North Carolina and wished her a happy Valentine's Day. After the last five years in Feyzabad, it still felt strange to be laughing and joking around in mixed company of my own age group.

Kabul's not so bad! I decided. *Country boy or not, I could live here. At least if Jeanne was with me.*

Little did I know the prophetic element in my thoughts. But however enjoyable the evening, I was also conscious the hours were slipping away. Tomorrow's weather prognosis was for clear skies, so another postponement of my flight home seemed unlikely.

I said good night to Jeanne with a heavy heart. I was still wrestling with what to do next. I didn't want to fly off the next day, leaving Jeanne to watch me disappear as I'd watched her slip away in that taxi the day we'd met. Especially with no idea when we might meet again and without having stated openly just how I felt about her.

The next morning, I called the ASI office as usual at 6 a.m. This time their response was different from the past week. "Yes, we're flying. Take-off is 8 a.m., so you'd better get right over here."

16: JOHN

HAVING ONLY A FEW ITEMS to toss into my bag, I'd been prepared to leave on short notice. When I reached the prefab hangar that was ASI's berth at Kabul Airport, a single-prop Cessna six-seater was warming up. By now Jeanne should be awake, so I called to let her know about the flight.

Her response was brief and composed. What was there to say? As the Cessna became airborne, I prayed for traveling mercies and tried to comfort myself with the view of the landscape unrolling beneath the aircraft's fixed wings. The flight was only a fifty-minute hop, and beige wrinkles of rising foothills soon gave way to snow-clad peaks.

We were approaching a high mountain pass the Cessna would have to navigate to reach Feyzabad when snow began to fall. The pilot looked over at me. "I'll do my best to land, John. But if this gets any worse, we're not going to have enough visibility."

The problem wasn't Feyzabad, which was down in a river valley, but the jagged crags we had to traverse to get there. The pilot made several attempts. The worsening blizzard kept tossing the tiny aircraft around until at last he shook his head.

"Sorry, there's no way we're going to get through this storm. Would you like me to see if we can land over in

Taleqan? At least you'd be on this side of the Salang Pass. Then maybe you could find local transport over to Feyzabad."

Taleqan was a small city on a flat plain almost two hundred kilometers west of Feyzabad in the province of Takhar. I'd worked in that region before 9/11 and still had friends there. But if I was going to be stranded a few more days away from Feyzabad, I knew where and with whom I wanted to be. I shook my head. "No, if we can't land in Feyzabad, let's just head back."

My emotions were on a roller-coaster as the pilot banked back toward Kabul. I was also breathing praises to God for giving me one more opportunity to spend time with Jeanne even as I recognized I was simply postponing another painful farewell.

I called Jeanne as soon as the Cessna's landing gear touched pavement. It was less than two hours since I'd informed her of my departure, and her tone held surprise. "Are you in Feyzabad?"

"No, I'm back in Kabul." I explained what'd happened. "Can I come see you?"

"Of course!" Her surprised tone had shifted unmistakably to joy.

I caught a ride in the ASI van. God had obviously given me this bonus time with Jeanne for a reason. She must surely know how I felt. When I arrived at the office, her expression left me no doubt she felt the same way about me. I had determined I would not leave again without officially declaring my intentions. Now I wanted to spend this unexpected extra day with Jeanne, not an entire group.

Yet taking Jeanne anywhere alone necessitated getting permission. This wasn't just showing respect for Afghan cultural norms or for Jeanne's reputation as a young, single woman, but also standard security protocol. Approaching the British couple Georg had left in charge of the team, I asked their approval to take Jeanne out on an actual "date" where we could sit and talk without interruptions.

Just to clarify, most Afghan restaurants are largely for men. If women do accompany their husbands, there are typically separate family sections for women and children or even closed booths so strange men cannot observe a woman eating in public.

But with thousands of expat contractors, military personnel, government agencies, and aid organizations flooding in after 9/11, numerous western-style restaurants and other amenities restricted to foreigners had sprung up all over Kabul. Since Jeanne had spent several years of her childhood in Thailand, I chose a Thai restaurant not far from the office where an expat couple dining wouldn't raise eyebrows.

We walked there, talking, sharing, and praying as had become our pattern. Since this was our first official date in a restaurant, I felt awkward and unsure at first. But spending time with Jeanne felt so comfortable, natural, and *right* that I soon lost my nervousness.

Before I knew it, we had lingered for hours over our late lunch meal. It was now close to evening, so I called a taxi to take Jeanne home. When we arrived, I paid off the taxi, planning to walk back to the guesthouse where I was staying.

Jeanne and I stood outside the gate. I could hear the chowkidar approaching. My heart was racing. I might not deserve someone like her, but this was my win-or-lose moment. I believed God had brought Jeanne into my life. It seemed she'd fallen in love with me as much as I'd fallen in love with her. But if I was wrong, if she just saw me as a good brother in Christ or just a country boy lost in the big city to whom she'd chosen to show kindness, I was about to find out.

God, give me courage! I prayed. Jeanne was looking up at me, the light of the street lamp illuminating her lovely features, her gaze questioning. The chowkidar was making noises on the other side of the gate. I took a deep breath. The words that came out were far from polished.

"Jeanne, I like you." Though I'd used the term "like", I hoped my tone conveyed what I really wanted to say— love. "These days together have been so special. I'd love to pursue a relationship with you. Who do I need to speak with to get official permission to keep seeing you and getting to know you better?"

17: JEANNE

MY HEART FELT READY to break as John and I stood outside the wall of the compound I shared with several female housemates. Back when I lived in New York City, I'd asked God to seal me away in a bubble, safe from the ups and downs of dating, until the time when the husband God had chosen for me came into my life. Now I was experiencing precisely such an up-and-down emotional roller coaster.

I could no longer deny that I was completely smitten. The more time we spent together, the more deeply I fell in love with John. Here was a man who fulfilled all my top priorities. He had a passionate heart for God and His global purposes. He was fully committed to loving and serving others, especially Afghans. He also loved to pray as much as I did. In addition, he was as courageous and charismatic as any Prince Charming. Every day of the past week, I'd breathed thanksgiving: *Wow, God, I can't believe You are blessing me so much! Thank You, Father God!*

Then doubts would flood in. Yes, John had sought me out every day since he'd arrived in town. But was I overreaching that he had a personal interest in me? Was he just filling time while he was stuck in Kabul?

After all, he'd never actually said how he felt about me or verbalized his intentions. We were always in a group, even when talking and walking back and forth from one place to another. And every day I knew this could be the last. When John called each morning, my heart leapt with joy that he was still in town. But every evening as we said goodnight, my heart plunged into desolation that these might be our last moments together.

Valentine's Day was a watershed point for me. I never received the note John had slipped into one of my shoes and only found out about it much later. There are typically dozens of shoes lined up at our office veranda. Perhaps it ended up in the wrong one or someone else picked up the note, thinking some admirer had sent them a valentine.

Since I didn't know about the valentine, I didn't notice John's preoccupation either. I simply took pleasure at being with him on this significant holiday. One advantage of living in Kabul was being able to enjoy mixed-gender outings as was impossible in other parts of Afghanistan. That evening, the men and women who had gathered together for dinner and karaoke were not just good friends but brothers and sisters in Christ. Yet as John and I sat beside one another, our companions clearly considered us a couple.

Then partway through the evening, John called his mother. With no self-consciousness, he put his cell on speakerphone and began singing the Stevie Wonder hit: "I just called to say I love you." He had a sweet singing voice, but his thoughtful gesture in remembering his mother on Valentine's Day is what tugged at my heartstrings.

I was also seeing another aspect of his character. We'd had so many serious discussions on spiritual matters, global affairs, and the needs of Afghanistan. This was a more lighthearted, playful side of John.

As he sang, a female colleague leaned over and whispered to me, "He's just perfect!"

I couldn't agree more. When the evening ended and we once again parted with a simple goodnight, my heart felt wrenched between pleasure and pain. Fervently, I prayed, *Father God, please don't let him go back to Feyzabad without saying something! My heart can't take much more of this!*

The next morning I received a call from John saying that he was boarding a flight to Feyzabad. I managed a courteous response, but I felt an emotional wreck. Though I kept my composure at our daily team meeting, inside I was crying out, *God, why are You letting this happen? I asked You to shield my heart from falling in love if this wasn't Your will for me!*

Calming down, I reminded myself that this was my Heavenly Father whose loving hand on my life I'd experienced too many times to doubt now. I bowed my head and will in surrender. *Okay, Lord, You know my heart. And maybe You have something else in mind here I just don't know about. But if this is what You are allowing for my life, then that's okay with me.*

Just a few minutes later, John called. Unbelievably, he was back in Kabul. Soon he was at the office making arrangements to take me out for Thai food, my favorite. At the restaurant we talked about everything under the sun and asked each other tons of questions. What do you think about this? What do you believe about that? It seemed we were of the same heart and mind on every topic we raised.

John escorted me home in a taxi. I didn't want the evening to end. Surely God must have a reason for bringing John back so unexpectedly today! The chowkidar was about to open the gate. Suddenly there was no more time. Would John let me go again with just a simple goodbye?

Then he was speaking. "Jeanne, I don't want our time together to end. I like you. Who do I need to speak with to get permission to keep seeing you and get to know you better?"

For such a gifted conversationalist, it wasn't the most polished proposition. But I didn't care because his awkward stumbling for words signaled his sincerity. His tone and the anxious hope that lit his green eyes conveyed all the words he had not said. *Jeanne, I'm falling in love with you even though I'm afraid to admit it. And I'd love to spend the rest of my life with you!*

A smile filled my heart so that it was instantly as light as a balloon. I knew John could read my reaction in my expression. "Georg. You'll need to talk with Georg."

Then the chowkidar was ushering me inside and John was walking away. As the compound gate shut behind me, I breathed a prayer. *Father God, thank You. John said it. You can send him back to Feyzabad now.*

18: JOHN

THE NEXT MORNING I awoke to bright sunshine. When I called the ASI office, they informed me Feyzabad had blue skies too. My flight was a go. Now that we'd formalized our courtship, I was ready to get home.

I called Jeanne as soon as I arrived in Feyzabad. This set a pattern for the coming weeks of regular phone calls to talk and pray together as well as lengthy emails to share our hearts in writing. We could now openly express our growing feelings for each other.

Jeanne was a pleasure to get to know. I cherished every moment like finding a priceless treasure. But I still wrestled with the life-long commitment of marriage. One day while sorting through tons of donated clothes for a distribution to needy families, I pleaded with God to help me with my internal struggle and to speak to me.

"Father God, is it *Your Will* for me to marry Jeanne?" I repeated out loud several times. Suddenly, a little green stuffed turtle fell out of the clothes bag I was sorting. As I picked it up, I saw words inscribed on the turtle's belly: *GO FOR IT*.

Okay, Lord, I get the point! I'd been acting like a shy, slow turtle. But now this was exactly what I needed to hear (or rather, read!). With this additional confirmation, I had complete confidence to move forward.

In Afghanistan, going through proper channels to obtain permission—whether of parents, employers, tribal leaders, town officials—is an important part of the culture. As followers of Christ who planned to serve long-term among Afghans, Jeanne and I were both in agreement to honor and respect their customs and set an example of a godly courtship. So I began a round of phone calls and personal visits to request formal approval for our courtship.

This included our parents and our NGO director as well as other organizational and spiritual leaders. Their response was unanimous support. I also shared with Afghan friends and colleagues as I valued their input and wanted them to feel included. They all agreed and felt a man my age was long overdue for a wife. Furthermore, they were interested in what kind of Kabul-born American bride I wanted to bring to Feyzabad.

As for Jeanne and me, I don't know just how or when our conversations turned to an assumption of a future together, even if nothing about marriage had been said. Sure, we'd both been praying for God's will. Yet after that brief exchange outside of Jeanne's gate, things happened so rapidly over the next few weeks that it felt like a dam breaking, sweeping us forward at whitewater speed.

The first event happened in late March when Jeanne flew up to Feyzabad to spend a few days. Feyzabad is far more conservative than Kabul, so an unmarried woman coming to see an unmarried man would be scandalously out of the question. But my friend David, whom I'd met with at that worship gathering last September, was flying up with his wife and children to visit one of our projects. Jeanne was able to travel in their company.

I was eager for Jeanne to see my home. After all, Kabul was a metropolis. Feyzabad was a mountain village with few amenities. I wanted her to experience our remote living conditions for herself.

We didn't have one unchaperoned moment together during that visit, certainly no private walks or meals. Yet we still found opportunities to talk and pray together. One occasion stands out. We'd taken a hike with David's family and others to the top of a nearby mountain ridge. From there we could look out over the entire valley. As Jeanne and I stood there together, praying God's blessing over Feyzabad and its people, someone took a picture of us, one we still prize.

"Can you see yourself living in a place like this?" I asked Jeanne.

"Definitely," she responded with sincerity. "It's beautiful as are its people."

My next words were to ask if I could have her parents' phone number. Even as she gave it to me, I knew she understood what this meant—that I planned to ask her parents for permission to marry her. Remembering Jeanne's story of how her parents had met and married in Africa, I hoped they wouldn't be too shocked at a man they'd never met from a place like Afghanistan asking to marry their only daughter.

When I did call them, Jeanne's parents seemed to know all about me. They gave their immediate consent and full blessing. Now how was I to broach the subject with Jeanne herself, especially since by this time she had already returned to Kabul?

The apostle Paul, in expressing his calling and passion to preach the Good News (Gospel) of Jesus Christ to all peoples, states: "*I have become all things to all people so that by all possible means I might save some*" (1 Corinthians 9:22 NIV). Paul is speaking of integrating into the local community, culture, and language—whether Jew, Gentile, or in my case, Afghan—without compromising faith in Christ in order to more effectively share God's Word and make disciples of all nations.

Similarly, I wanted my courtship of Jeanne, along with our engagement and wedding, to honor as much as possible the local culture that had become my own while at the same time being a life-giving witness of our faith in Jesus Christ as well as His incredible love and passionate pursuit of His own Bride.

With that in mind, I asked several Afghan friends how I might go about proposing marriage in their culture since I had no family here. They explained that in some traditions here on the ancient Silk Road a bridegroom would typically purchase a scarf as a sign of a marriage proposal.

Since their own marriages were mostly arranged, the bridegroom's mother would actually present the scarf to the intended bride and her mother. If the young woman's family accepted the proposal, she'd take off her own scarf and wrap the bridegroom's gift around her head and shoulders, signifying her willingness to become his bride.

But I had no one to act as a surrogate mother. So I purchased the finest silk scarf I could find and made arrangements with our driver to travel overland to Kabul. Another expat colleague who had some business in the capital went with us. This was the second week of April, and while snow still cloaked the mountains, fresh green life was springing up everywhere. We stopped for meals and lodging at various *chaikhanas*, a combination tea shop/motel (caravansary) to meet the needs of weary travelers.

Even as I journeyed, consumed with passion to seek my own bride, I didn't forget the purpose for which God had brought me here. As was my practice everywhere I traveled, I took time to stretch out open hands to thank God and pray His blessing over our meals and those around us. This led to inquiries and dialogue about why I, a foreigner from the godless west, would pray to God like a good Muslim.

On other occasions, my colleague and I would begin a conversation with each other, referencing a story from the Holy Book (God's Word). Afghanistan is not a shy culture, and Muslims are very religious. So inevitably someone listening would ask a question that would lead to deeper discussions. God's Word tells us to always be ready to give an answer for the hope that we have in Christ, with gentleness and respect. (1 Peter 3:15).

I also carried in my vest copies of the Dari New Testament as well as DVDs of the Jesus Film. A long discussion with one chaikhana owner led to giving him a copy of the Jesus Film. Somewhat to my own trepidation, he immediately loaded the film into a DVD player hooked up to a TV. Since not all there might be so approving of a movie about Jesus Christ, I quickly suggested to my companion that we hit the road before any trouble erupted.

I arrived at the guesthouse during the team prayer time. I hadn't told Jeanne I was coming, but I did coordinate with Mrs. Irene, the guesthouse hostess, since I would need her assistance. When prayer meeting was over, Mrs. Irene discreetly arranged for Jeanne and me to sit in the living room.

As she served us tea, I carefully flattened out across my lap the plastic package in which the scarf was wrapped.

19: JEANNE

WHAT A RELIEF TO NO LONGER have to hold in my feelings about John! My friends and colleagues certainly took note of my bliss. One day I was in the kitchen cooking with my Swiss housemate and colleague, Claudia, when my cell-phone rang. Busy, I let it ring, figuring if the call was important, they could leave a voice message or call back. Glancing at the phone, Claudia said, "You're going to want to take this one."

Moving closer, I saw the name *John Weaver* blinking on the screen and immediately snatched up the phone. We both had busy work schedules, but somehow managed to squeeze in hours of phone calls and email letters.

Now that our courtship was official, I contacted my friend Sue in NYC, to let her know I was dating the author of the book she'd given me. I also called my parents to rave about the man with whom I'd fallen in love. "If you want to know who he is, just get his book *Inside Afghanistan* and read it."

My parents did so. Not long after, my mom called me back. I could hear her choking back tears. "What a great guy! Or should I say, quite a remarkable young man as Peter Jennings states in that quote from him on the book cover. And John's pledge at the end to serve the Afghan people as long as God gives him life—remarkable indeed!" Needless to say, my parents were fully supportive and impressed with John even before meeting him. And that has never changed.

Feyzabad was an eye-opener, beginning with the flight in. The landing field was a narrow steel-grate runway laid down by the Soviets that looked and felt like rumble strips. Next to a paved slab for unloading stood a crumbling, hollowed-out shell of a building that still bore a sign announcing "Airport Feyzabad." The town was tiny compared to Kabul, its dusty market district just one street, the surrounding landscape barren of vegetation. The amenities at the compound where we stayed were sparse.

But I didn't care because John was there and that was all I needed to make the place my home. It was a busy week of NGO work, being hosted for meals at different expat homes, never alone for a moment. Yet John and I had learned by now to carry on our own dialogue of shared glances, conversations with our own subtleties, or moments stolen for a murmured exchange during a group hike. When John asked me for my parents' phone number, I knew what he was really saying.

Still, I wasn't expecting John to walk into the Kabul guesthouse less than two weeks after our rendezvous in Feyzabad. While Mrs. Irene poured tea, I noticed John had spread a package out on his lap. I had some idea it must be a gift for me.

But once Mrs. Irene left us alone, John didn't immediately open it. Instead, he began talking about Afghan marriage customs. I'd already learned that John was a natural teacher at heart. He liked to set things in context, explaining their history and significance as well as present-day practical application.

He was always interesting, so I enjoyed listening to his explanations. But today I was anxious to know why he had come so out of the blue and what was so special about that package. By now he'd opened it, so I could see its contents—a silk scarf. He was explaining that in some Central Asian people groups a man gives a scarf to the woman he wants to marry. If she puts it on, she is accepting his marriage proposal.

Then he handed me the silk scarf. I admit that seeing John so unexpectedly had affected me, since only then did it sink in *why* John had traveled all this way to surprise me and *why* he'd spent so much time telling me about various cultural practices.

Instantly tugging my own scarf free, I joyfully wrapped his gift across my head and shoulders.

20: JEANNE

IT DIDN'T TAKE LONG FOR the news to spread that we were engaged. John ended up staying in Kabul a few days because our Afghan colleagues insisted a marriage proposal wasn't complete without an official Afghan-style engagement party. In the end, we had three of them. They all shared one thing in common—candy. In fact, the Afghan word to describe these parties means "to eat sweets."

The first was thrown by our NGO staff, the group with whom I'd spent the most time since coming to Afghanistan. Outside the expat team, most of our local staff were Pashtun males, many of them former mujahedeen. Tall, powerfully-muscled men with long, bushy beards, they had looked fierce and even scary to me upon initial acquaintance. But I'd learned what softhearted, kindly personalities lay behind their fierce exterior. They treated me like a daughter, and all felt invested in making sure this John Weaver was a suitable bridegroom.

Mari, an older Afghan woman on staff who mothered all of us younger single women, insisted on planning the engagement party according to Afghan custom. She arranged with my chowkidar for John and me to shop for rings and new clothing worthy of an engagement—a light-blue *shalwar kameez* and white round hat for John and a purple outfit and scarf for me. Mari also arranged for a decorated cake and ribbon-wrapped implements.

Our Afghan engagement ceremony was similar to an American wedding minus the official pronouncement as husband and wife followed by a kiss. In front of witnesses, bearded Afghans and our expat team members, John and I exchanged rings. Arms linked, we drank a ceremonial toast of Fanta soda and cut the cake. A memorable moment came when one Afghan rose to his feet and asked, "If something happens to this marriage, who is going to stand up for Jeanne?"

The significance of this in Afghan culture is that every woman lives under someone's protection—their father, husband, or other extended family. If death or even divorce dissolved a marriage, a woman without such protection would be left destitute. These Afghan colleagues knew I was alone in their country without the protection of father, brother, or uncle.

Mari rose to her feet. "I'll stand up for Jeanne."

"I will too," several other staff chimed in. I felt wrapped with love. In a land where I had no family, these had become mine.

We celebrated a second engagement party with a house fellowship of Christ-followers. At the end of the regular worship time, the Tajik pastor brought John and me forward for prayer. This was followed with a cup of tea and the distribution of candy or sweet refreshments. Expatriate colleagues and friends planned the third engagement party that also included candy, along with pizza and prayer for God's glory in our upcoming union.

After our engagement parties, John flew back to Feyzabad. So I wasn't expecting to see him on my birthday, which was April 30th. Catching a ride down to Kabul with a friend, he showed up at my door with flowers. Shamelessly, he got down on one knee in the street outside my gate. A wide grin lit up his face and his green eyes twinkled as he said, "We got engaged with the silk scarf, but I never officially asked—Jeanne, will you marry me?"

I couldn't do anything but smile. "Yes, I'll marry you! Now get up! People might be watching us."

Throughout this time period, one topic routinely arose with our Afghan acquaintances. I'd explained in the past that I was still single because my father hadn't yet given approval of a bridegroom for me. It was one reason for a grown woman remaining unmarried that made sense in their culture. Most Afghan weddings were arranged, so it wasn't uncommon for a bride and bridegroom to meet for the first time at their engagement party, if not the wedding itself.

Afghans were curious as to whether ours was an arranged marriage or a love match, such as they'd heard about in other cultures. John and I came up with a simple, but truthful answer. Our marriage was indeed arranged, but not by our earthly parents. Yes, our parents gave their full blessing, permission, and support. But it was our Heavenly Father who'd brought us together so unmistakably it couldn't be by mere human arrangement.

Our marriage was also a love match. While God had designed and destined our relationship, God had also given us a deep desire and love for each other. Interestingly, this was the part Afghans found most fascinating. For an Afghan bride, the wedding is usually filled with sadness. Often she is literally torn from her mother's embrace, then carried off by a total stranger, who may be much older than her. So tears were expected from a young wife-to-be and even considered a sign of parental honor and respect as well as innocence and purity.

To not just know about each other, but to actually want to be together out of mutual love and trust was a new, intriguing concept to many Afghans. So they were naturally curious. What would a wedding between two Christ-followers be like? Perhaps that was where the inspiration for getting married in Afghanistan first sprang to life.

21: JOHN

I LOVE THE AFGHAN PROVERB, "The walls have mice and mice have ears." News, especially secrets, can spread like wildfire.

Due to my years as an aid worker as well as authoring *Inside Afghanistan*, I had acquaintances, both Afghan and expat, all over the country. Within days, it seemed that many of them had learned of my engagement, especially within Feyzabad. Now they wanted to know when and where I was going to marry my chosen bride.

I would have been happy with tomorrow. But all kinds of complications and unanswered questions arose as Jeanne and I began talking about the actual timing for our wedding. We hadn't yet met each other's parents. Should we plan a trip for introductions? Where would we get married? Especially since Jeanne's parents were currently stationed in Amman, Jordan. Should Jeanne fly back to the U.S. and make arrangements there?

I don't remember how soon our talk shifted to the option of getting married in Afghanistan. Perhaps as soon as I realized that the simplest solution to traveling stateside, meeting family, or dealing with the logistics of our responsibilities in Feyzabad and Kabul would be as a married couple. Granted, I wanted to claim my bride as soon as possible, but sheer practicality also made our continued separation senseless.

Yes, we'd only been in each other's company for a few weeks. But this was Afghanistan where couples routinely met on their wedding day. By that standard, Jeanne and I were far ahead of the curve. If an engagement period meant further separation, what was the point? Why not marry here and get to know each other better after the wedding like any Afghan couple?

Perhaps I was thinking too much like an Afghan. On the other hand, I wasn't unaware of the obstacles. Had there ever been a Christ-centered wedding here? Was a marriage of Christ-followers even legal inside Afghanistan?

Despite the overthrow of the Taliban regime, Afghanistan remained an Islamic government where the local mullahs (religious leaders) controlled every aspect of the judiciary, including marriage. I and our NGO had built a good reputation for all the relief and development projects that benefited countless Afghans. But the city and district leaders were all devout Muslims who might find a public wedding of two disciples of Christ quite offensive.

Nor were the possible consequences of such a reaction negligible. The Taliban might be gone, but some of their attitudes were not. Strict Islam still ruled, especially in a conservative region like Feyzabad. Over the last several years since the Taliban were overthrown, the security situation for aid organizations, embassies, ISAF personnel, and private contractors had been fairly good. But I was hearing the first rumblings against the foreign influx that in time would erupt into a renewed and brutal civil war.

Would an openly Christ-centered wedding put my bride or even our organization in needless danger? Certainly over the following weeks, some well-meaning people would tell us so!

Nevertheless, the more Jeanne and I fasted, prayed, and talked, the more convinced we became that this idea came from God, not our own longings. After all, this wasn't just the place to which God had called me, but also the place where Jeanne herself had been born. It was the land of our shared calling. We were committed to living here long-term. Where else should we get married than among the people and in the place that we called home?

More than that, God had called us as Christ-followers to be the salt of the earth and the light of the world. We wanted our union to be a testimony of God's passionate love for the people of Afghanistan as we vowed our love to each other. We also knew that our wedding wouldn't just be a witness to those who attended. As the proverb goes, the walls have mice and the mice have ears!

As Jeanne and I continued to pray and seek God's will, we came to the same assurance that this was the initiative of God and that He was indeed calling us to marry and without further delay. In fact, we were so convinced that we decided to get married twice—first in Feyzabad and then in Kabul.

On the other hand, this wasn't just our decision. I've mentioned the importance of seeking permission in Afghan culture. Many times with Afghan men, I'd be asked religious questions. Always, I'd look to the oldest gray-bearded elder in the room and ask, "*Ijosa ast* (is there permission)?" Only when the elder nodded consent would I respond with an answer, a clarifying question, a proverb, or story from the Bible.

Honoring their cultural practices had contributed significantly to developing close relationships with the powers-that-be in Feyzabad, who were all well aware that I was a fully devoted follower of Christ. And unlike our engagement, getting approval from parents, team leaders, and spiritual advisors wouldn't be enough. If we were to marry in Feyzabad, all the civic leaders, along with the entire community, would need to be on board.

After several dozen, I lost count of the number of permissions I ended up having to acquire—some by email, others by phone, while others necessitated a face-to-face hearing. Our parents were easy, although none could come to our wedding. My parents were just happy that I'd found someone crazy enough to marry their nomadic son. As for Jeanne's parents, they were hardly in a position to criticize our choices when they'd done the same to their own parents.

"Well, what can I say?" Jeanne's mom responded wryly when Jeanne called to seek their approval of our desire to be wed in Afghanistan. "You are your mother's daughter, definitely a chip off the old block."

We also sought the input and prayers of our international friends. We were conscious that any backlash over our wedding could affect other believing expats and their organizations. They were overwhelmingly supportive, though a few did express concerns.

Our Afghan friends expressed no doubt at all. Marriage in their culture was a practical transaction, and they saw no reason for delay. They expressed feeling delighted and honored that we would consider holding our wedding in their country. After all, we weren't foreign tourists after some exotic "destination" wedding or other self-promotion.

Didn't Najiba-jaan's parents work in Kabul during the reign of King Zahir Shah? Hadn't Najiba-jaan been born in their country? And wasn't John-Agha ("Agha" is a title of respect) a faithful servant-leader and member of their own community?

When some less friendly radicals raised objections, insisting Christ-followers like me shouldn't even be allowed to stay in Afghanistan, the local elders would respond, "Where have you been these last seven years when our people needed help? Don't you know everything John-Agha and his organization have done for our people?"

I still had to get permission from the governor, mayor, district attorney, and military commanders, along with other civic and community elders. I also had to check with my own embassy as to the legality of two Americans getting married on Afghan soil.

A final issue to decide was timing. The end of the school year in June was when many expats left the country, whether traveling during the summer months or moving on permanently to a new posting. I myself had a book signing and speaking tour planned for Australia in August. We could wait until the fall. But the Tajik pastor whose fellowship Jeanne worshipped with in

Kabul and several other good friends we wanted to participate in our wedding were all leaving in June.

Our other alternative was to get married before the summer rush. But we also wanted to make sure our NGO director, Georg, would be back in-country for the wedding. The only open week that worked for everyone was the last week of May.

To this day, I am in awe that Jeanne agreed, considering this was just six weeks from the day I proposed to her with that silk scarf. Now we had less than a month to pull off two weddings in two different locations in the not-so-easily traveled terrain of Afghanistan.

We decided on Tuesday, the 24th of May, 2005, for our Feyzabad wedding and Sunday, the 29th of May, for our ceremony in Kabul.

First picnic together at the King's Garden in Kabul.

Our first engagement party with local staff.

Jeanne arrives in Feyzabad as John sings *Isn't She Lovely*.

Together on the tarmac, the day before the wedding.

Prayer-walking and planning the week-long celebrations.

Henna on Jeanne's hand that will unite with John's.

Breakfast on the verandah with bridal party.

Here comes the beautiful bride.

Afghan ladies watching from nearby roof.

Unity candles to show that two become one.

A love marriage filled with joy and laughter.

Bowing and praying at the Kabul wedding ceremony.

Giving thanks before cutting the gigantic wedding cake.

Afghan-style portrait at the Kabul Green Wedding Hall.

Kissing John Mack while picking tomatoes in our garden.

Team Weaver: (back row) John-Agha & Najiba-Jaan (front row from left to right) Yusuf, Injila, Yaiyah, Eshaq.

22: JEANNE

HOW COULD WE PLAN two separate weddings in less than a month? More so, one would be an outdoor ceremony in a remote northeastern mountain village and the other an indoor one in the centrally located capital city. Both would need to weave together elements of American (western) and Afghan (eastern) culture in such a way that would give glory to God without unnecessary offense to our adopted countrymen. Without lots of prayer, God's miraculous intervention, and the diverse team God provided us, it would not have been possible.

John was up in Feyzabad making arrangements with the community there. Most of the Kabul preparations fell to me. Thankfully many Afghan and expatriate colleagues and friends pitched in to make sure Najiba-jaan and her bridegroom had a proper celebration.

For example, Dan had been a florist back in Manila, the capital of the Philippines. Enthusiastically offering his expert assistance, he asked about my wedding theme.

"An Afghan wedding," I said with a smile. "I was hoping you might help with decorations and flowers."

So Dan created a beautiful bouquet as well as decorations by clipping flowers from gardens of various friends and team members. He even picked my wedding colors and arranged for a gigantic cake to feed up to 500 people.

Our NGO's Afghan receptionist took on the task of researching various wedding halls for us. There is no such thing as a "Christ-centered" or church wedding in Afghanistan since there are no Christian church buildings. Wedding halls, however, are a major industry in the capital city with all sizes, prices, and levels of flamboyant gaudiness. Expecting about five hundred guests, we booked an entire floor at the Kabul Green Wedding Hall.

Next was my wedding outfit. In Afghan culture as in America, a wedding dress is usually white, symbolizing purity, prefaced for the preliminaries by a green outfit, indicating virginity. I found exquisitely-embroidered and bedazzled traditional Afghan outfits in blue and green for my wedding journey and bridal festivities. But how could I find the perfect wedding dress in such a short time?

Here, in a memorable way that illustrates our Heavenly Father's sovereignty and unconditional love, my mother stepped in. While in college, I'd traveled to see my parents, who were once again stationed in Thailand. One day I accompanied my mother to a fabric sale, where she took a shine to a ten-meter roll of snow-white Thai silk, insisting it would be perfect for a wedding gown. I made it clear I didn't expect to need a wedding gown any time soon and maybe not at all. Regardless, she purchased the fabric anyway.

My mother is a gifted seamstress. So when she learned there was a reason to unearth the silk after fourteen years of being in storage, she was overjoyed. Her challenge wasn't just the short time frame. Along with beauty, the outfit had to conform to Afghan cultural norms—long-sleeved, high-necked, and loose-fitting with a veil. My artistically gifted Swiss housemate Claudia quickly went to work with my mother to choose a design, sending countless emails back and forth.

The final choice was an elegant Italian design with a pearl-and-sequin-embroidered French lace overlaying the Thai silk sleeves, a multicultural mix that seemed fitting for a bride who'd grown up all over the world in a Foreign Service family. My mother, aunt, and grandmother worked feverishly to complete it, FedExing it to New York City just in time for my friend Sue to hand-carry it by plane to Kabul. The story was so unusual my mother was asked to write an article for the June/July 2013 edition of Vogue Patterns magazine, titled "A Wedding Gown for a Distant Land."

John and I talked every day to pray and discuss progress, especially our planning for the ceremony itself. We wanted as many Afghan features as possible while still making it clear we were pledging our union before the one true God of Abraham, Isaac, and Jacob. We chose specific Bible passages, spiritual rituals, and songs. We also decided that the two of us would take Holy Communion as our first act of worship after being pronounced husband and wife.

Mark, an ethnomusicologist who wrote original Dari worship music, led a musical group that played Afghan instruments. He actually took on the task of providing music and instrumentalists for both weddings. Georg, our NGO director, committed to flying with me to

Feyzabad to walk me down the aisle, an actual red carpet in this case.

An Iranian pastor would share from the Holy Bible and pray God's blessing over us as a local religious leader might do. Kurt would pronounce us husband and wife since he was a licensed clergyman in the United States. There'd be no American-style maid of honor or bridesmaids, but Mari, Sue, Claudia, Gulbahar, and other close female friends would take the place of the mother, sisters, aunts, and girl cousins who made up a traditional Afghan bridal entourage.

In all of this, I kept myself too busy to think. I clung to those evening calls with John as a reminder that this was the man I loved and with whom I desired to spend my life. But I was also beginning to panic.

At thirty-two, I was accustomed to doing things my way, being independent. Now I was about to merge my life with a man I'd spent far less time with than any of my male Afghan colleagues. Moreover, this would happen in a culture where a wife literally belonged to her husband, her only duty to please him and bear children.

I knew John didn't drink coffee, preferring green tea. It was also obvious he loved God and desired to serve the Afghan people. But I was beginning to realize how little else I knew about this man who was soon to become my new "authority figure" and carry me off to the faraway and isolated northeastern mountains.

Had I heard God? Or was I crazy to be jumping into this so quickly? And once we could spend time getting to know each other, what if John didn't like who I turned out to be? After all, who was I that someone I admired, loved, and respected so much would be interested in spending the rest of his life with me?

My doubts became strongest in the dark hours of the night. I found myself getting up at three to four a.m. to pour out my concerns to my Heavenly Father. The first hour I'd spend panicking more than praying. Gradually, the Holy Spirit's calm, quiet voice would get through to me, reminding me of all the ways God had made it clear that John was His choice for me. Including that jolt when I first saw John's picture on the cover of *Inside Afghanistan*. By 7:30 a.m. when I needed to head over to the team prayer meeting, I'd be at peace again.

John and I compared notes later. He had also been waking up at that same hour to intercede for our union. My turmoil lasted all the way until the day of our wedding. Where this fits into normal pre-wedding jitters, I don't know. But every day I had to make the choice to cling to God's promises and revelation regardless of my emotions.

I might not yet know John well, but God knew everything about John even before He knit him together in his mother's womb. God also knew me and loved me. So if our Heavenly Father had chosen John and me for each other, I'd simply have to trust that it was for His greater glory and our good and that all would be well.

23: JOHN

I HAD NO DOUBTS at this point about marrying Jeanne. I still had to remind myself that marrying such a marvelous woman was not some dream. Not that I had much time for dreaming, much less tossing and turning on my narrow cot. In fact, I had far more work than I was sure I could pull off before my wedding day. This was a reminder that I also needed to add to my to-do list finding a proper bed for my bride before our wedding night.

I'd already made arrangements with ASI to fly Jeanne and her entourage up to Feyzabad on May 23rd. But the biggest part of the wedding plans was the mid-day meal we'd need to serve to all the VIPs and a good segment of Feyzabad's male population on the day of the wedding. We were expecting to feed at least a thousand people, so rounding up enough manpower along with the rice, carrots, raisins, lamb, oil, and other ingredients to make *palau* was a challenge.

The ceremony itself would be held in the compound courtyard. We'd scheduled this between the mid-afternoon and sunset calls to prayer so as not to inconvenience our majority-Muslim guests. One thing we couldn't control was the weather. We prayed daily that God would orchestrate the much-needed spring rains so as to permit an outdoor wedding.

In a traditional Afghan wedding, I'd be getting married at my father's house and preparing a place there to receive my bride. The necessity of providing for a dowry, wedding costs, and a dwelling place is one reason Afghans often have to save up for years to get married. I had no family home in Feyzabad to host my wedding, so in a sense I and my senior Afghan co-workers were playing the role of father, preparing "my" house to receive my bride.

Arrangements were well underway when one of my Afghan colleagues approached me. "John-Agha, I'm curious. Where are you and Miss Najiba going to be husband and wife?"

Mystified at his question, I gestured toward the compound courtyard. "You know we are holding the wedding right here."

"No, not the wedding ceremony," he insisted. "Where is the room you're getting ready for your bride? You know I am also engaged, so I am preparing a room in my father's house to receive my bride. If you are to be married this week, you must have a special place prepared for Miss Najiba-jaan."

His words hit me like a sunbeam bursting through a cloud. How many times had I heard and even repeated similar words from Scripture? The passage was from the Gospel according to John, when Jesus had comforted His disciples over His upcoming death on the cross, His resurrection from the dead, and then His departure back to heaven:

Let not your heart be troubled; you believe in God; believe also in Me. In My Father's house are many mansions; if it were not so, I would have told you. I go to prepare a place for you. And if I go and prepare a place for you, I will come again and receive you to Myself, that where I am, there you may be also.

—John 14:1-3 NKJV

Jesus had spoken these words to men living in a culture similar to Afghanistan. I was struck by the parallels to my own upcoming nuptials. Jesus had left His disciples to return to His Father in heaven, just as I had left Jeanne to return to Feyzabad. But Jesus hadn't abandoned or forgotten His followers any more than I had Jeanne. Just as I was working hard to prepare for my bride, Jesus is also preparing a place for His Bride in His Father's house. One day Jesus will come again in glory to gather His Bride from every nation and carry her off to spend eternity with Him in the heavenly home He has prepared.

A magnificent spiritual insight, but it didn't help me figure out just how I'd provide my own bride with a honeymoon suite. Thankfully, several of my Afghan colleagues told me, "Do not worry about it, John-Agha. You are as family. We will prepare the room with our wives as though you were our own son."

As mentioned before, our NGO base was actually two adjoined compounds, one with a red house, the other with a green one. The green house would be designated the women's quarters, since men and women were kept completely segregated at Afghan weddings. The red house had a larger courtyard and a wide covered veranda in front, so that was where we planned to have the wedding ceremony. On the second floor, right above where we'd be pronounced husband and wife, was the room my Afghan friends would prepare for us. I was incredibly thankful—and busy—enough I didn't inquire too closely as to the details.

Preparations were now as complete as possible. God willing, ASI would be touching down with my bride in the morning. I decided it might be a good idea to check out our honeymoon suite in advance.

Stepping inside, I found a scene out of an Arabian Nights movie set. Flowered drapes in rich reds and greens flowed down over the windows. The floor was covered with a colorful new carpet, also various shades of red and green. All other furnishings had been removed, and in the center of the carpet was the bridal bed.

This was similar to a typical *tushak*, the long bolster cushions Afghans used for sleeping or lounging. But the material covering this one was green velvet. While as long as a twin mattress, it was only half the width. It was also much higher, a good two feet tall. I'd find out that with use it would squash down and spread out to normal size. But now I just stared, wondering how two people could possibly fit—much less keep from falling off.

There were no pillows, but an ornate flowered bedspread adorned its bulk. Sprinkled across the bedspread and the carpet were rose petals, cut flowers, candies, and chocolates.

If nothing like I'd imagined, it looked wholly Afghan. In any case, it was too late to think of changing it for something more familiar even if that were an option after all the hard work my Afghan friends had invested into creating this bridal chamber.

I'd just have to trust that Jeanne would be more joyous than stunned when I took her to the place prepared for her!

24: JEANNE

WE HAD ARRANGED FOR two ASI flights to transport the wedding party to Feyzabad on Monday, the 23rd of May, the day before the wedding. The first flight was all the men along with the cargo and two seventy-pound duffle-bags full of gifts Sue had brought from family and TSC friends—clothes, candles, perfume, cologne, candy, and other goodies. I flew up on the second flight with my female entourage.

I vacillated somewhat nervously on what to wear since I had no idea what—or who—would be awaiting us at the Feyzabad Airport. Typically an Afghan bride-to-be would be hidden while traveling under a full burqa. I chose an elegantly-embroidered peacock-blue Afghan dress that was floor-length and loose-fitting, its matching scarf long enough to wrap around my arms and torso as well as head and shoulders.

Sue, my friend from NYC, was also enjoying the experience of Afghan dress in a long skirt and scarf. My entourage and I made quite a multicultural assembly. Claudia was Swiss and Harriet Dutch. Gulbahar was Tajik and Bekah Iranian. We were all friends from the worship gathering I attended. Mari, my Afghan mother figure, was the only married woman in our traveling group.

As the small plane's landing wheels scraped over the airfield's rumble strips, I could see at least a dozen vehicles through the window. Not to mention, an entire crowd gathering to meet us, at a glance all male. Nerves knotted my stomach. Was I modestly covered enough to step out in front of all those men?

Lord Jesus, please help me glorify You, I began praying silently. *Don't let me make a mistake that will embarrass John or hurt his reputation!*

As the plane taxied over to the unloading slab, the engines went silent. Part of the fuselage unfolded to become steps downward. One by one, my female entourage exited the plane. Sue as my chaperoning "sister" deplaned just ahead of me. Clasping tightly the bouquet of red and pink roses my Filipino colleague Dan had created for me, I ducked through the plane doorway. It was time to face the music.

The noisy jostling and stares of strange men, many with cameras and video camcorders, was as nerve-wracking as I'd anticipated. Then I saw John stepping away from the crowd to greet me. Wearing the sky-blue *shalwar kameez* and scarf my chowkidar had helped us pick out, his tight curls freshly-trimmed and bare of hat, he looked as handsome as any bridegroom could. But it was the pure pleasure on his face when he saw me that calmed my heart.

Then, in his less serious-minded and more spontaneous side, John began to sing another Stevie Wonder classic: "Isn't she lovely, isn't she wonderful?" This time, he was singing in Dari, his entire male companions smiling and cheering him on. Torn between amusement and blushing embarrassment, I could do nothing but smile myself as he reached my side.

From this enchanting moment, the rest of the day was dreamlike, all lingering doubts swept away. Having been to Afghan weddings, I'd had a secret desire for one of their customs: the bridal car and caravan.

Since an Afghan bride is to some extent a purchased commodity and the bridegroom's family hosts the wedding, ensuring the bride's expeditious delivery is a sensible precaution. But it is also reminiscent of biblical times as the Lord Jesus referenced in His Parable of the Ten Virgins (Matthew 25:1-13) where the bridegroom comes in a procession to claim his bride and carry her off to his father's house for the wedding feast.

The bridal car was not an official request, rather what I referenced earlier as one of my "half-prayers." A simple wish expressed to my Heavenly Father like riding on the back of that bike with John. With all John had to do in such a short time to prepare our wedding, I hadn't even thought of such a possibility. So I felt even more cherished and treasured when John led me over to a white four-door sedan covered in the streamers and flowers of a bridal car.

Ushered into the back, John and I weren't able to exchange more than a few murmured words. But just sitting side by side was enough for now. Georg climbed into the front seat beside the driver, then swiveled around to train a camcorder on us. Reviewing that footage now, we both look googly-eyed with glee, unable to stop grinning and eyeing each other.

As we drove into town, all the other vehicles and their passengers fell into a caravan behind us, honking so loudly that residents rushed into the streets to watch us pass, all aware that John-Agha's bride had finally arrived. Somewhere in that caravan was the rest of my entourage, but I was so focused on John I didn't really notice.

The bridal car finally turned into the main gate of the double compound where John lived. To my right, I could see the red two-story house with its wide covered veranda where the wedding would take place. Straight ahead was the mudbrick wall with a small pedestrian gate that led into the parallel compound with its two-story green house that had been designated female territory. My entourage had arrived as well, and we were guided through the pedestrian gate to the "women's quarters." That was the last I saw of John that day.

The next hours were spent unpacking, getting rooms ready to sleep that night, and preparing for the Afghan version of a bachelorette bash—the henna party. It was too noisy and I was kept too busy to even think of what John might be doing on the other side of the wall.

By evening our side of the compound was filled with women and children. A few were fellow Christ-followers, many of them expats working in Feyzabad. The majority were wives and other female family members of city officials, NGO staff, and others curious to check out the bride, Najiba-jaan, and her entourage.

While the women and children gathered in the green house's largest salon, my entourage was preparing me upstairs. Claudia, who had helped design my dress, took charge of my hair and makeup. I wasn't accustomed to wearing makeup or fancy hairdos. So I felt as though I'd been decorated for a famous model's photo shoot by the time they were done with me.

Evening had fallen by the time the bridal festivities started. As with the wedding ceremony, John and I had prayed and talked about how we could incorporate God's Word into the henna party.

To kick off the festivities, Mari danced into the main hall, a long room furnished only with floor rugs and tushaks around the walls. Accompanying her was my Iranian friend, Bekah, who carried in both outstretched hands a Holy Bible, nicely wrapped in cloth as a sign of reverence. Then the rest of my bridal entourage swept me into the room.

Once I as the bride was settled in a place of honor, Mari gave a welcome and explained that we would first read from the Holy Book and then give thanks to God. After reading God's Word, my Tajik friend Gulbahar led in prayer. She has a passionate faith, and her praying is equally passionate. She poured out her heart in praise and thanksgiving, asking God to bless Najiba-jaan and John-Agha, our wedding, this city, and all the families and ladies in this room.

In Islamic tradition, most prayers are memorized recitations. But this was different. By the time Gulbahar finished, the expression on these women's faces made it clear they'd been deeply impacted by the personal nature of Gulbahar's direct communication with Almighty God.

Then Mari, with lovely Afghan humor, described the displayed wedding gifts from John, our family and friends in a show and tell like fashion. And that was all we had planned before the Afghan meal and henna painting.

Suddenly everyone's eyes turned to me. I had no idea what to do. Leaning over, Claudia whispered, "You need to say something!"

"No, the bride is supposed to just sit and be quiet!" I whispered back.

Which was true, except an Afghan bride was also supposed to have a mother who'd be speaking on her behalf. Making the decision that bridging this awkward silence was more important than sticking to strict Afghan protocol, I began to speak. I thanked everyone for coming and expressed how honored I felt to be making my future home here. I then introduced each of my friends who had accompanied me from Kabul.

As I did so, it suddenly struck me that the women in this room would be a big part of my new life once I married John. These were the wives, sisters, daughters, aunts, grandmothers of his colleagues and friends. In a society where I'd be restricted largely to female company, these would also become my own associates and—hopefully—friends as well.

Gratefulness welled up in me. I began silently praising God. *Father, thank You for this new home to which You've brought me and for these people You've made part of my life!*

The rest of the evening, I played the proper silent role of an Afghan bride. A feast of rice and meat was served. Women began dancing and singing, their choreography making evident Bollywood had reached even these distant mountains. But the central part of the evening was decorating the bride.

Henna is a dye made from dried leaves of the henna plant. Applied to the skin, it creates a temporary tattoo.

It has been used for centuries throughout Asia and the Middle East to create intricate skin designs.

It is also a traditional part of beautifying a bride for her husband. One of the Feyzabad women who'd come to welcome John-Agha's bride took charge of my henna decoration. Placing my left palm upward on my head, she began with a large dot in the center of my palm, then added a simple pattern of dots and lines. Wrapping a cloth tightly around the designs, she explained that I was to leave my hand bound all night.

Throughout all this, the festivities displayed one stark difference from a traditional henna party. An Afghan bride is supposed to be silent above all because she is supposed to exhibit sadness and fear of marriage. In contrast, I couldn't keep from smiling. Somewhere on the other side of the compound wall was my bridegroom, and my heart overflowed with joy and thankfulness that in just a few hours I'd be his bride.

The dancing, singing, and feasting went on late into the night, but as the bride I was dismissed early to get my "beauty sleep." The room prepared for me and my entourage was little different than the hall downstairs, carpet on the floor and tushaks for sleeping mats. As I curled up on a tushak, carefully cradling my wrapped hand so as not to smear the henna designs, I prayed for John, for the preparations going on next door, for tomorrow and all the tomorrows to follow that we'd spend together for God's glory.

With heart fluttering and mind racing, I wondered if John was as eager and excited as I was.

25: JOHN

I COULDN'T REMEMBER FEELING this blessed and stressed at the same time. The high moment was welcoming my fiancée to her new home. I wasn't dreaming. She was actually here. This was really going to happen. Soon we'd be husband and wife.

Once Jeanne disappeared into the women's side of the compound, pressure slowly began overtaking my joy. An enormous amount of preparation remained for feeding a thousand-plus people for tomorrow's noon meal. I ran around, trying to delegate as much as possible, but also gathering supplies, setting up necessary items, even taking a turn at cutting up vegetables. Then I discovered to my dismay that we didn't have enough water for a thousand guests, not just for cooking and washing, but for clean drinking water and making tea.

Feyzabad had no water source of its own except the Kokcha River, which ran through the town, and a system of narrow, shallow canals that only held water during the rainy season. A huge reservoir had been built at the top of a mountain ridge overlooking the city to collect water from the spring rains and melt snow.

This reservoir was strictly regulated. The water was piped to different parts of the city each day, where residents would line up at neighborhood faucets to fill their water containers. The spigot in our neighborhood was dry, and we weren't scheduled again until the day after the wedding.

Ironically, our NGO had been involved in helping the local municipality maintain and expand the reservoir system. While I was praying about our predicament, God prompted me to ask the mayor for help. Whether out of appreciation for our years of service or because he planned to be at the wedding himself, the mayor immediately put in a phone call.

Within a short time, water was running in our neighborhood. In the meantime, I'd mobilized every able-bodied man on the property, along with a few neighbors, to collect as many water kettles, buckets, jerry cans, and barrels as possible. By the time we'd filled and hauled them all to the compound, I was exhausted.

But I still had to make an appearance at my own henna party. This was a much smaller, shorter event than the women's festivities, mostly local staff, neighbors, close friends, and a few expatriate colleagues. The main part was decorating my right hand with henna, the most important part of the design being a large dot in the center of my right palm.

The significance of the henna was that the bridegroom and his bride would join hands at a point in the wedding ceremony, bringing together the two dots as a symbol of union. I don't remember all the details. We sang a song, danced, and someone prayed a blessing over me. Then as soon as my henna design was wrapped, I went back to work till late in the night.

I have no idea when I finally got to bed, but I slept only a few hours before returning to work in the morning. Jeanne and her entourage left early to spend part of the day at a coworker's home so we could use both compounds to prepare food and receive our lunch guests. The men handling the meal dug several pits for roasting lamb and cooking rice to make the national dish—*palau*. In the courtyard, we laid down carpets, then rolled out rose-colored plastic to create a dining area.

Indoors, we spread vinyl tablecloths on the floor in every salon for hosting guests. On the walls, we hung decorative posters featuring various favorite Bible passages in Dari, such as the I Corinthians 13 passage about love. Mark and others with musical and technical skills were setting up loudspeakers and getting music ready for background entertainment.

Another concern had arisen by now. With the wedding celebration taking place outdoors, we'd been praying for clear skies, but the day had dawned overcast. As the morning advanced, clouds heavy with moisture closed in overhead and a comfortable breeze became a brisk wind.

Some were murmuring that the darkening sky was a bad omen. Others argued that in this dry, barren land a rain shower signified God's blessings and provision. All we could do was pray and hope that any serious rain would hold off until after the wedding. Or at least not disrupt the ceremony.

By noon, the rain was still holding off. Guests began arriving by the hundreds, including the governor, minister of foreign affairs, and many other city elders and government officials as well as many former Northern Alliance commanders and their mujahedeen entourages. Most had known me when they were fighting the Taliban and I was helping internally displaced persons (IDPs). They also knew I was a follower of Jesus Christ and that I cared deeply about the Afghan people. Today they had come to show their support of John-Agha finally taking a bride.

Both courtyards were packed by 1 p.m. While there wasn't much time for spiritual conversations, I saw many guests reading the Bible passages on the walls. I'd greeted and escorted to indoor seating countless VIPs when one of them approached me to express concern. A *very* important person hadn't come to the party. A powerful general in Massoud's Northern Alliance army who had been one of the most feared military leaders. He was also the brother-in-law of our landlord as well as a close relative of the mayor.

My own acquaintance with the general came under rather dicey circumstances. It had been early 2004. Mark, who was doing the music for our wedding, had recently joined our team. We'd gone on a hike to the top of the highest mountain overlooking the area, a trek dotted by landmines and rusting Russian tanks. Mark had brought along a small guitar. When we reached the peak, we paused for a time of praise and prayer over the city.

Abruptly, a mujahedeen soldier had come running up the trail, his AK-47 cradled and ready to fire at us.

Fortunately, I'd learned enough Dari to understand what he was screaming at us.

"What are you doing up here? Don't you know this is the general's high place? No one else is permitted up here!"

The soldier marched us back down the mountain along a different trail than the one we'd hiked up, traversing a cemetery dotted with green flags signifying fallen mujahedeen. As we were ushered into the general's compound, he came out to meet us. One of his arms looked debilitated, possibly from a war injury. Despite his ruthless reputation, the general was quite ordinary in appearance, of average build, and soft-spoken. Ordering chairs to be brought out for us, he asked what we were doing on his mountain.

I introduced Mark and myself, explaining that we were humanitarian workers. I mentioned some of the projects we'd done before 9/11 and what we were currently doing to help his province. I also explained that we were followers of Isa al-Masih (Jesus Christ) and had been worshipping Almighty God up on the mountain, interceding for the Lord's peace over the city and its people.

The general looked taken aback but nodded his satisfaction. "Okay, then. Thank you for what you are doing to serve my people. If I can help, just let me know."

We left, feeling as though we'd just grabbed a lightning bolt unscathed. From that point on, the general was friendly and cooperative with our activities. Since liberation, he'd grown increasingly wealthy, acquiring additional wives and keeping a finger in every legitimate or illicit pie in the zone. A good cross-section of government ministers and officials owed their positions to him and/or were his family members. He was widely considered to be the real ruler of the region.

I don't recall having noticed the general's absence. Though somewhat surprised, I wasn't worried. I just assumed he had some scheduling conflict or more important business. But other VIPs were now questioning why he hadn't come. It could be taken as dishonoring or a deliberate insult if he didn't make an appearance at John-Agha's wedding.

Or was he making an intentional statement by boycotting even the feast of a Christian celebration? If I hadn't at first been concerned, I could now see that some of my friends, including several community elders, felt a sense of shame and were both alarmed and upset at the general's absence.

"John-Agha, you do realize he might be one of the only men in town who hasn't come to your party," they told me. "This isn't good!"

Our landlord, the general's brother-in-law, got on the phone. Sure enough, the general was at home. "Why have you not come to John-Agha's wedding feast?" The landlord demanded.

His phone call worked because within fifteen minutes the general was strolling in the gate with his armed soldiers. Mark and I personally escorted him and his top aides to the nicest salon in the house. It just happened to be the room with a poster of the Ten Commandments.

While I was arranging for food to be brought, the general walked over and started reading the Bible passage. Considering he was breaking most of those commandments on a regular basis, I braced myself for his reaction.

But as Mark and I sat and ate with him and his mujahedeen, he began asking questions with genuine interest. "So these are God's commandments from the Holy Book? How can any of us keep such laws?"

"Yes, they are God's laws," I replied. "And it is true that none of us can perfectly keep all of God's laws. This is why we need God's forgiveness, grace, and mercy in our lives. And this is why we follow Jesus, the Savior of the world."

Mark and I were able to briefly explain the contrast between God's saving grace and trying to earn salvation through keeping the law. We also prayed God's blessing over the general, the city of Feyzabad, and the entire Badakhshan province. He then said his goodbyes and left.

That was just one of many such discussions or questions about faith arising throughout the day. In more ways than one, our prayer that this wedding would be a bright light and shining witness was already coming to fruition.

The Sovereign Lord seemed to be in complete control, which is another reason why that spiritual attack in the washroom caught me off guard. Looking back, it shouldn't have been a surprise. Satan doesn't like to see God's children forming holy, Christ-centered marriage relationships and godly homes. Much less to see the light of the Gospel of Christ penetrating the darkness of territory he has long held captive in his unholy grip.

Some might dismiss my crisis of belief in the bathroom as the result of stress and exhaustion. But I know whose lying voice I heard that day. Moreover, I know how the Holy Spirit restored faith and peace to my soul.

I left the washroom clothed not only in my brand-new white-gold shalwar kameez, but in the full armor of God, fearless and zealous for the culmination of these last hectic weeks—claiming my bride as my own in the sight of God and man.

26: JEANNE

BY MORNING, ONLY MY BRIDAL party remained in the green house. We breakfasted on naan bread and tea. Then John showed up to escort us to an expat friend's home until the all-male part of the marriage feast was complete.

The walk over was the only time John and I had spent together since I'd arrived, and it felt far too brief. But it was sweet to walk side by side, praying together as one. I knew how much was on his shoulders in the coming hours. As soon as he left, I gathered my entourage to pray for John and all the activities of the day.

Once the lunch guests emptied out, we returned to the women's side of the compound, and I began my own preparations. Throughout, I continued praying for John. I knew what we'd planned for our wedding ceremony might be considered controversial in this conservative stronghold.

John was the one who would be doing most of the speaking. I prayed that God would anoint him and give him just the right words. I also prayed for my own role— that I'd bring glory, honor, and blessings to my bridegroom and my Heavenly Father through my words and deeds.

I did feel curiosity as to the honeymoon quarters I knew John had arranged. Thus I asked Claudia to check it out just so I could prepare my own reaction when I saw it. She came back with a positive report: "It's Afghan but beautifully and romantically set-up." That left me reassured but even more curious.

By mid-afternoon I was ready in my Thai-silk wedding gown and veil. At which point I was settled in the middle of the courtyard like a queen, except that my throne was a wooden schoolroom desk chair. Many women from last night's henna party as well as wives, daughters, and smaller children of the men who'd attended the wedding feast were crowding into the courtyard to catch a glimpse of the bride.

Trapped behind the curved school desk, I couldn't even interact with the ladies and girls. Then I decided to invoke my foreign status and break with Afghan bridal protocol. Getting up, I began approaching each guest to greet them individually.

For many of them I was a novelty, not only because John was so well known, but because they'd heard I was marrying my bridegroom for love. So they wanted to see if I really looked as happy as had been rumored.

Before long, the threat of rain became a reality. I had to retreat to cover to keep from spoiling my bridal attire. My entourage and I huddled together to pray that the rain would lift before the ceremony. It didn't, but neither did it worsen into a full downpour. Since delaying the ceremony risked running into evening call to prayer, the decision was made to go forward as planned.

By the time my entourage disappeared to take their seats and Georg as "father of the bride" arrived to escort me next door, the rain had settled to a slight sprinkle. I didn't let the weather dampen my joy. Whatever happened, the next hour would see me becoming the wife of John Weaver. Nothing else mattered.

27: JOHN

WHILE I'D BEEN GETTING ready, the other NGO staff had been working hard to clear away the debris of feasting, replacing the plastic dining cloths with chairs and benches from the classrooms. We couldn't do much about the ongoing drizzle, but the loudspeakers up on stands had been draped with plastic for protection.

The veranda was actually a wide stone terrace running the width of the building that rose a good two meters above the courtyard, its roof held up by square pillars. There Mark had set up his musical instruments, a sound system, microphones, and a video camera. A low table at the front was draped with a shimmery-green cloth, upon which were set out candles, the elements for Holy Communion, and some candies.

Lining the wall behind the table were chairs where the bride and bridegroom would sit along with those participating in the ceremony. A nicely wrapped Holy Bible was on a small shelf we'd mounted on the front wall. A red carpet had been laid out from the veranda to the pedestrian door linking the two compounds, where Georg would emerge with the bride.

Despite the dampness, the courtyard was already filling up with several hundred of our lunch guests who'd returned for the wedding ceremony. Before long the seating was filled, and even more men as well as young boys jostled each other along the walls and back of the compound. A mushroom patch of unfurled umbrellas protected against the light rain.

Visible above the compound walls was a sea of blue where women had crowded onto adjoining rooftops to watch the festivities from under the cover of their burqas. I was thankful to see that many local VIPs and dignitaries had returned for the ceremony. One group huddled under a single large umbrella included the mayor, district attorney, and minister of education.

Kurt, who would officiate our actual union, had also arrived with his wife and children. Kurt had counseled, encouraged and prayed much for me during our courtship. So I felt privileged and honored that he'd be the one pronouncing us husband and wife.

As the courtyard filled, Mark on his harmonium along with his other musical companions began their playlist of Dari instrumental music. The loudspeakers carried the music over the walls, attracting even more viewers to rooftops and windows, especially when Mark started singing a famous national song by the late Ahmad Zahir, who was like the Elvis of Afghanistan.

Occasionally, Mark would include a Dari worship song he'd written or one translated from English that would be unfamiliar to our local audience but that followers of Jesus would recognize. We'd chosen one such song as the bridal march.

When all was ready and Jeanne's entourage emerged from the women's side to take their seats up front, Kurt and I took our own seats on the veranda. Standing up, I briefly welcomed our guests to the bridegroom's "home." I also gave greetings from both of our families and a bit of context about our celebration. Then Mark shifted into an instrumental rendition of "This is the Day that the Lord Has Made."

At that signal, the door opened. First emerged young girls with baskets filled with rose petals, which they scattered along the red carpet. Then Jeanne and Georg stepped into view. Georg was dressed much like me in an embroidered silk shalwar kameez, but a lighter cream shade, covered by a formal suit coat.

But I wasn't looking at Georg. I hadn't seen the wedding dress Jeanne's mother had fashioned or Jeanne herself since that brief walk in the morning. Even under a headscarf and enveloping Afghan dress, Jeanne had always been beautiful. But at this moment, standing tall, glowing, and graceful in the white silk of her wedding dress, she took my breath away.

Clasped in front of her, Jeanne held a bouquet of red and pink roses, its ribbons cascading over her hands. Small, white flowers were bound into her hair. From them a veil of sheer, thin netting spilled over her head and shoulders, doing nothing to obscure her face or hair while preserving the expected proprieties that in an Afghan wedding would have the bride completely cloaked from the gaze of strange men.

Jeanne walked slowly towards me, her sandals releasing a delicate perfume as they pressed down on the rose petals. By now, everyone not yet standing had risen to their feet. A murmur swept through the crowd as they took in the sight of this glorious, radiant bride.

Few of these men had ever seen the face of each other's wives or female family members, much less so stunning a wife-to-be. Certainly this part of our wedding was one they'd never forget.

28: JOHN

THE NEXT HOUR FOLLOWED the outline we'd planned in advance. As Jeanne took her place at my side, the music stopped and the crowd settled down. Then the Iranian pastor stood up. He took the Holy Bible from the shelf, ceremoniously unwrapped it, and kissed the cover. This is a gesture of reverence dating back to biblical times when a synagogue leader would bestow a kiss on a scroll of the Holy Scriptures before unrolling it.

Turning to the New Testament, the Iranian pastor read 1 Corinthians 13, known as the "love chapter." I was acutely aware that most of this audience had never heard such inspiring words, much less in context of how a bridegroom should love his bride:

> Love is patient, love is kind. It does not envy, it does not boast, it is not proud. It does not dishonor others, it is not self-seeking, it is not easily angered, it keeps no record of wrongs. Love does not delight in evil but rejoices with the truth. It always protects, always trusts, always hopes, always perseveres. Love never fails.
> —1 Corinthians 13:4-7 NIV

The pastor explained how each of these characteristics is true of God, but is also how God calls us to treat one another, especially our spouse. Sharing the story of creation from the Bible, he went on to tell how God had fashioned the first man, Adam, and from his own DNA created a helpmate for him, Eve, the first woman. Explaining how this was the first union of husband and wife, he then read Christ's own words about marriage:

> For this reason a man will leave his father and mother and be united to his wife, and the two will become one flesh. So they are no longer two, but one flesh. Therefore what God has joined together, let no one separate.
>
> —Mark 10:7-9 NIV

He continued to speak of God's design for marriage. A bridegroom and his bride were to love each other and come together in a holy union that should never be pulled apart by anger, quarrelling, or divorce. I could see from facial expressions that this description of marriage sounded strange and even bizarre to most. But occasional nods among the audience indicated a yearning to experience such a loving relationship.

Then Kurt took over. His role followed closely the traditional western wedding ceremony. He asked who gave permission for this woman, Najiba-jaan, to marry this man, John-Agha. Then Georg spoke the customary words of a father surrendering the bride to her bridegroom.

Next we went through the "do you take this woman as your wife" and "do you take this man as your husband" part. We also added the local ceremonial response that translates as "I give myself completely to you."

Here again we followed the Afghan custom in saying each statement and repeating our response three times. It was another reminder of how many traditions here stretched back to biblical times when repeating a promise three times signaled a commitment that couldn't be broken. Jesus Christ after His death and resurrection had asked Peter three times if Peter loved Him, and three times Peter avowed his love (John 21:15-19).

Kurt then handed me the microphone so Jeanne and I could exchange our own vows. Looking into Jeanne's eyes, I passionately poured out my heart: "Najiba-jaan, I love you. I receive you as God's precious gift to me. I promise to love you as Christ loves the Church and to lay down my life for you as Christ laid down His life for us. I promise to never leave you, forsake you, or divorce you. I promise to never abuse you, hit you, or mistreat you in any way. I promise to serve you all the days of my life."

Even as I expressed my feelings with all the strength in me, I wasn't unaware of the whispers of the crowd. My vows to my bride were very different from what an Afghan husband considered his rights over his wife—not only to hit her or punish her if she angered him, but to cast her forth with a simple declaration of divorce three times over, once for each time he'd pledged to take her as his wife.

As I was declaring my vows, I did hear some rumbling, so I turned to the crowd with a dramatic smile, asking, "Is it not right what I've said?"

Whether they fully agreed or not, there were cheers and applause. Then I handed the microphone to Jeanne. Her vows were similar. After all, in Afghan culture, a wife's commitment to serve and obey her husband wasn't in question.

Looking into my eyes, she spoke with deepest affection: "John-Agha, I love you too. I also accept you as God's blessing and gift to me to be my husband. I fully commit myself to you and promise to be your faithful wife all the days of my life."

Once we were pronounced husband and wife, Jeanne and I knelt down at the low table that had been placed at the edge of the veranda. Before us were two tall, slim, pale-blue candles with a larger matching one in a glass receptacle. There was also a chalice of grape juice and a plate holding a piece of unleavened bread. As was customary in a typical western wedding, we first lit the two long candles, then together lit the larger "unity" candle to show how two become one.

We still had the crowd on our side, murmuring approval of this love marriage, even if it was unlike their own. But the next part of the ceremony was what might be too controversial. I prayed silently even as I reached for the elements of Holy Communion. I knew Jeanne and others were praying too. Though addressing my words directly to my own bride, I was also communicating to our entire listening audience.

Nor was I speaking just to those in the courtyard or those crowded on surrounding rooftops or even those listening in the streets to what was being broadcast on the loudspeakers. One aspect of Afghan culture is the popularity of wedding videos. It is not uncommon to use the video of a family wedding or that of a friend to entertain guests. Perhaps thousands more would eventually witness our celebration through the video that was being recorded.

In fact, we eventually learned that both Mark's music from our wedding and the video itself had been pirated for sale in local bazaars. In some remote villages where water turbines powered enough electricity for a single TV, the two most popular community "movie nights" became the Jesus Film and John-Agha and Najiba-jaan's wedding video.

Even at the moment of taking Holy Communion, I was again reminded that the walls have mice and the mice have ears. Whatever we said and did here today, as well as in our Kabul wedding, would be like a stone of remembrance that in biblical days would be set up as a reminder of our great God's awe-inspiring deeds for the next generation. So we'd determined that if we were to hold a Christ-centered wedding, we should clearly and courageously proclaim the Good News of Christ.

Picking up the bread, I looked into Jeanne's eyes, speaking slowly yet loudly for all to hear. "Najiba-jaan, it is an honor and privilege for me to become your husband and for us to worship God together in this way. We believe that in the beginning Almighty God created the heavens and the earth, including Adam and Eve, placing them in the Garden to become the very first husband and wife.

"Sadly, Adam and Eve did not obey God's command. Through their disobedience, sin and shame entered the world, destroying mankind's relationship with God. Yet God promised He would restore that relationship, and all the prophets—Noah, Abraham, Moses, David, Isaiah, and others—have sought to help mankind come back to God."

To this point, I knew I had my audience on board since their own religious teachings also spoke of God as Creator, the Garden of Eden, Adam and Eve, humanity's fall, and God sending prophets. As I continued speaking, however, I was stepping out onto more controversial ground.

"All the prophets foretold of the promised Messiah who would come to restore our relationship with God and let us experience His redeeming love. As the Holy Book tells us, at just the right time the eternal Word of God became a human like us. Jesus Christ was indeed born of the Virgin Mary and lived a perfect life. He spoke God's Word, forgave sin, and healed the sick. He also gave sight to the blind, made the lame walk, and even raised the dead. He showed God's grace, love, and power."

If some chatter swept through the crowd at the mention of the Messiah and His miraculous life, it wasn't yet restless. After all, they knew we were followers of Jesus Christ. Didn't the Quran also speak of Isa al-Masih as the greatest of prophets, born of the Virgin Mary, sinless, and performer of many miracles? But I was not finished yet.

"We know Jesus Christ is the holy Lamb of God who shed His own blood on the cross as the perfect sacrifice to take away the sins of the world. After He suffered to pay the penalty for our sins, He was buried in a grave, and on the third day He rose again to prove He is indeed the eternal Son of God, the Savior of the world. Through His death and resurrection from the dead, He conquered the devil, death, and hell so that we no longer need to fear them. He also destroyed the curse and power of sin, removing our guilt and shame so that we can experience forgiveness and fellowship with Almighty God, our Heavenly Father."

Then I broke the bread. "Before Jesus Christ died for us, He took bread and broke it, saying, 'This is My body given for you; eat this in remembrance of Me.'"

Jeanne and I shared the bread. Then I lifted the cup. "Isa al-Masih also took a cup of grape drink, saying, 'This cup is My blood of the new covenant, poured out for the forgiveness of sin; drink this in remembrance of Me.'"

I continued on, "Jesus instructed His disciples to eat of the bread and to drink of the cup to proclaim His death on the cross until He comes again. Our Lord commanded us to do this. So in faith and obedience, that is why we share Holy Communion here today for the first time as husband and wife."

Once we'd drunk from the cup, I grasped Jeanne's left hand in my right hand, where our adjoining henna spots symbolized the union God had pronounced over us. Together we raised our hands, and I poured out my heart filled with thanksgiving and intercession.

"Almighty God, thank You that You love us. Thank You for making a way for us to return to You through the sacrifice of Christ whose blood was shed on the cross to rescue us from sin. Thank You that the Lord Jesus was raised from the dead with all authority, honor, and power to save us. And thank You, Heavenly Father, for Najiba-jaan, the wife You've given me and that we can worship You this way."

I concluded by praying for God's blessings on all those here today, friends, neighbors, Feyzabad, its leadership, as well as the country of Afghanistan. By the time I was done, all was silent. What the mayor, district attorney, and other government officials were thinking, I could not guess. But no one had yet walked out of the wedding.

Kurt and the Iranian pastor then moved forward to anoint us with oil. As they did so, they explained, "This oil represents God's Holy Spirit. As we anoint John-Agha and Najiba-jaan, we'll pray God's blessing over their marriage, the children God will give them, and that they will be a blessing to others."

A few others who'd been asked in advance also came forward to pray. We wanted men and women as well as several languages to show that the God we serve is the One True Living God of all humankind. Kurt started in the local dialect, then the Iranian pastor in Farsi, next Georg in Pashto, followed by Harriet and Jeanne's Tajik companion.

Their prayers were different from rote, memorized ones, demonstrating a real personal relationship with God as our Heavenly Father. Even those who might not have understood every word looked awed that anyone could talk directly to the Creator of the Universe with such child-like faith and intimacy. This was another compelling witness of the greatest love story of all.

By the time they finished praying and giving thanks, any restlessness roused by my homily had subsided. Throughout the ceremony, there were also the songs we'd chosen. After Holy Communion, Mark had played and sung one of his own Dari compositions, its lyrics lifted from the last book in the Bible, Revelation, chapters four and five:

Holy, holy, holy is the Lord God Almighty . . . You are worthy, our Lord and God, to receive glory and honor and power . . . Worthy is the Lamb that was slain, who has redeemed us by Your blood from every nation and tribe.

Then Mark began another of his own compositions, based partly on the prophecy of Isaiah, chapter sixty:

Arise, shine, for your light has come, and the glory of the Lord rises upon you. See, darkness covers the earth and thick darkness is over the peoples, but the Lord rises upon you and His glory appears over you. Nations will come to your light, and kings to the brightness of your dawn.

This melody was much faster and upbeat. Immediately, the audience began clapping. We'd debated whether we should include any dancing, which would be the norm in an Afghan wedding. But in mixed company and with our small window of time, we'd opted for discretion.

On the other hand, it just didn't seem an Afghan wedding with no dancing at all. So as the crowd clapped to the beat of the music, I jumped to my feet and did my own dance, shimmying Afghan-style with enthusiasm that displayed my delight, rejoicing over my bride.

If any tensions remained from the obvious Christ-centered ceremony, the timing of Mark's music along with my spontaneous twirling around Najiba-jaan proved the perfect ice-breaker. In most Afghan weddings, the party would have continued throughout the night. But I was conscious of the need to wrap up before the mosques began sounding their call to prayer.

I also didn't want to wear out our welcome. It was possible we'd drawn more attention than might be prudent or expected by some of our friends. As host, I brought the ceremony to a close, thanking everyone for coming. I also expressed the honor of being allowed to get married here in their country—the birthplace of my wife. I then acknowledged the mayor in a gesture of respect.

Here was his opportunity to show any displeasure with how we'd conducted our ceremony. God's Spirit had been so obviously with us throughout the whole day that I felt neither fear nor nervousness. But I did hold my breath a bit as the mayor stood to speak. Thankfully, he was smiling and added only a few phrases, offering his own well-wishes and gratitude to all who'd come.

Then it was over. The courtyard slowly emptied out. Jeanne's entourage, other expats, and local NGO staff picked up the equipment, chairs, and other paraphernalia. Then with a flurry of blessings and congratulations, they all left as well.

Taking Najiba-jaan by the hand, I led her upstairs to the bridal chamber, the place prepared for her. For the first time ever, I found myself completely alone with my bride. I felt my heart overflowing with the poetry of another long-ago bridegroom:

> Arise, my darling, my beautiful one, come with me. See! The winter is past; the rains are gone. Flowers appear on the earth; the season of singing has come, the cooing of doves is heard in our land. The fig tree forms its early fruit; the blossoming vines spread their fragrance. Arise, come, my darling; my beautiful one, come with me.
>
> —Song of Solomon 2:10-13 NIV

29: JEANNE

I WENT THROUGH THE CEREMONY in a daze of euphoria and nervousness, praying silently that I'd offer no offense to the watching phalanx of Afghan officials. I was also interceding for John, whose role was so much greater and potentially provocative. Our only communication was exchanged glances and our vows. But that was enough to radiate our mutual joy. When John took my hand in his warm, strong grasp, henna against henna, I felt like a bride deeply loved, valued, and fully claimed.

The rain tapered off gradually during the ceremony so that umbrellas were furled and tucked away. Then towards the end, something spectacular happened. The lowering, gray clouds lifted and parted so that the sun emerged, filling the compound with bright light and turning the surrounding brown, rain-drenched hills to sparkling gold. I knew our Afghan guests would see this as a good omen. For me the sweet, gentle rains watering the parched earth and God's light piercing the clouds were a double confirmation of God's blessing poured out on our wedding.

When it was all over, John led me upstairs. The room he'd prepared was as unusual and certainly as Afghan as Claudia had hinted. I found it alluring and romantic like the harem quarters prepared by some Arabian Nights royal prince for his Scheherazade.

Even more desirable and handsome was my own bridegroom. Finally we were all alone, and my heart cried out, "I am my beloved's and my beloved is mine" (Song of Solomon 6:3).

30: JOHN

OUR HONEYMOON NIGHT ended far too early with loud knocking on the door downstairs. Rolling to a sitting position, I caught sight of the time, 7 a.m. The disruption wasn't unexpected, but this was one part of the Afghan tradition I would have been happy to skip.

Like most Eastern cultures clear back to Old Testament times, it wasn't just the wedding ceremony that made a marriage official, but the actually joining together as husband and wife. So the morning following a wedding ceremony, family and friends would come around to the "father's house" to offer their congratulations. Most would bring blessings and gifts now that the marital union was consummated.

At least Jeanne could roll over and go back to sleep since the early arrivals were all men. As the commotion downstairs got louder, I scrambled into my clothing. Mark, who was staying on the other side of the compound, had volunteered to be up early to help receive guests. Like a family member would, he'd prepared our hospitality room with thermoses of hot tea along with a selection of candy and almonds spread out on a tablecloth in the center of the room. As soon as he spotted me, Mark broke into a wide grin. "John, your clothes!"

Glancing down, I discovered that in my hurry I'd pulled my *shalwar kameez* on inside out. I ducked back upstairs and corrected my dress. By the time I returned, Mark was welcoming the mayor, our landlord, and other community elders. Sitting on the tushaks, they all seemed friendly as they drank tea, nibbled refreshments, and chatted. Yet I could sense a certain stiff reserve or tension in the air.

After a round of greetings, one of the city elders, a former mujahedeen commander, finally brought the conversation around to their concern. "John-Agha, I'd like to share something. We just want you to know that we do not believe Jesus Christ is the Son of God who died on the cross to save us from sin."

It was precisely this truth that we'd known might rouse hostility. The hard expressions and murmured agreement in the room were indeed worrisome. These men knew I was a Christ-follower. They'd heard me share my faith before. I'd prayed for some of them or other family members in their homes. A few had seen the Jesus Film and even requested Bibles from me. So I knew not all were as adamant as this mujahedeen commander who'd raised the protest. After five years with these men, I'd learned not to argue or try to defend myself, so I just sat there quietly.

It was Mark, also experienced and wise in this culture, who spoke up with a smile. "Yes, yes, we hear what you say. But you know, we can all agree on one thing—we'll never have a better neighbor than John-Agha."

Immediately, his words diffused the tension. Nodding with smiles, they began reminding each other of the many contributions our organization and I had made to help their people. Now calm, they drank their tea, expressed their blessings and congratulations on my marriage, and soon left.

Later, I learned that one of the local mullahs, who'd refused to attend our wedding, had berated the community leaders, demanding, "How could you let this foreigner have a loudspeaker to proclaim the Gospel of Isa al-Masih through the streets of our city?"

Some of the men in that hospitality room had stuck up for me, telling the mullah tersely, "Now wait a minute. John-Agha might be a foreigner and a follower of Christ, but he has been here longer than you and done far more for our town. He is the best neighbor we've ever had."

For the moment, that was the main opposition we encountered over our wedding. However, in time some of the seeds of hostility the commander had voiced that morning would bear more negative fruit.

31: JEANNE

LATER IN THE DAY, wives of John's Afghan acquaintances and other female visitors came to congratulate me as well. I received them in my own separate hospitality room over in the green house that was the designated female quarters. John and I knew any real honeymoon would have to wait. The following days were busy, not just with receiving visitors but finalizing plans for our Kabul wedding. We also spent time in prayer and worship with our wedding party and other followers of Christ in the city.

There were also times for walks with John. We explored my new home and just enjoyed being together. Public displays of affection, even between married couples, weren't part of the culture. So when we occasionally walked hand-in-hand, people would stare. They smiled as well, intrigued by these crazy foreign newlyweds so openly in love with each other.

One day as we were strolling past the house of the district attorney, who'd had a front-row seat to our wedding, he emerged with several of his children to greet us. His grin grew broader as he noted our clasped hands. Jokingly, he said to John, "You know, John-Agha, you promised that you'll never hit your wife, but she never promised she wouldn't hit you!"

He then turned to me. "We all witnessed John-Agha's vow never to hit you. So if he ever does, you come tell me!"

His humor and the hospitable reception from so many town people made me feel welcomed and eager to make my home here with John. But first we had to complete our wedding festivities. On Saturday, May 28th, we all flew back to the big city. The next evening, Sunday, May 29th, we held our second wedding on the top floor of Kabul Green Wedding Hall, an ornate building of glass and chrome.

Luxurious wedding palaces, some as flamboyant and derivative in architecture as the Las Vegas Strip, were a growing phenomenon in Kabul's post-war reconstruction. A wedding feast for a thousand guests could cost a bridegroom's family more than $20,000 in an economy where the average salary for most Afghans was still less than $200 a month. This often put an enormous strain and massive debt on newlyweds, an excess on which the Afghan government was actually trying to crack down.

We'd picked a lower-priced location and menu. Our Kabul wedding was modest by Afghan standards with just over five hundred guests. This included some of Kabul's expat community, NGO colleagues, as well as hundreds of Afghan friends from the capital and surrounding provinces.

Georg had left the country after our Feyzabad wedding, so another older mentor, Gordon, took his place as my father figure. Dan had again arranged the flowers as well as a cake big enough to serve five hundred guests. Mark expanded his band and included a group of singers.

We'd still share our vows, light unity candles, partake of Holy Communion, and be anointed with oil. But this time our dear friend the Tajik pastor would proclaim God's Word.

Since this was at a wedding hall in the big city, both men and women attended. Several sections of a wooden partition about six feet high ran down the center of the room, safeguarding proper conventions with men and women sitting on opposite sides while granting both a clear view of the stage. At the end of the ceremony, we removed part of the partition to make room for Afghan-style dancing.

Two additions to our Kabul ceremony were serving the gigantic cake and sharing gifts. After we cut the cake, John made an announcement: "Thank you so much for coming. It has been a great honor for Najiba-jaan and me to have our wedding celebration in Kabul where she was born. We'd like to give you a gift. If you like the music you've heard, we have copies of the CD. You've also heard us read from the Holy Book, and we have some copies to share if you'd like one."

Many of our guests were happy to receive a Bible and a CD. Like our Feyzabad ceremony, the Kabul wedding became another stone of remembrance declaring Christ's sacrificial love and zealous pursuit of His own Afghan Bride. Our wedding DVD also spread through the bazaars as well as Mark's music.

Another ripple effect was the numerous Afghans who expressed how much they wished they could have such a wedding that conveyed mutual love and joy between a bridegroom and his bride. Throughout Afghanistan and in other diaspora locations, many Afghans have told us that they watched our wedding video and what a blessing it was to them.

At the time, we didn't fully recognize what a miracle it was to not only host twice over one of the first overtly Christ-centered weddings in Afghanistan, but to do so with such a sense of safety and security that all too soon would be a thing of the past!

32: JOHN

OUR KABUL WEDDING CELEBRATION was over. A local staff member drove us to the Intercontinental Hotel, made famous as a base for news media and diplomatic brass during the American invasion after 9/11. Along the way, our driver addressed us over his shoulder with some marital advice. He was a former mujahedeen fighter, a huge man—six feet, five inches and broadly built—with an enormous, bristling beard. We smiled at the contrast between his gentle, fatherly tone and fierce exterior.

The next afternoon we flew to Dubai for our "real" honeymoon. As soon as we arrived, I found a barber to shave off my beard. Jeanne had never seen me clean-shaven. Neither of us had seen each other in shorts or a bathing suit. For a few days, we enjoyed being just another newlywed couple—holding hands, sitting in the sun, walking the beach, splashing in the ocean, going out to restaurants, and spending hours alone together.

Then we flew on to Jordan, where I finally met my in-laws. They welcomed me as a second son. Jeanne and I also explored Jordan, visiting Petra and sleeping under the stars in a Bedouin camp.

We even journeyed over into Israel for one night. Our crossing was at Israel's most southern point, the port of Eilat on the Red Sea. The border guards were reluctant to let us in because our passports were full of visas from countries hostile to Israel, not to mention Jeanne's place of birth, Afghanistan. But after many questions and several hours, they finally let us cross.

We hadn't realized it was the Feast of First Fruits (a Jewish holiday) until we tried to book a room for the night. As we wandered from hotel to bed-and-breakfast to inn, we were reminded of another couple, Joseph and Mary, walking this sacred land who "found no room in the inn" (Luke 2:7) as they prepared for the first coming of Christ. Thankfully, before we had to resort to a stable or open field, a hotel clerk told us of an elderly woman who often rented lodging in her home nearby.

After some searching under the scorching sun, we found the house. This was a handful of tiny rooms built around a small courtyard that was filled with farm animals and birds. The landlady, Bianca, showed us to a narrow cot in a closet-sized room, its walls too thin to drown out snoring on the other side. Still, it was shelter and more comfortable than what our Savior's earthly parents had the night of His birth.

The next day we crossed back over into Jordan. Driving to Amman, we boarded a flight to Afghanistan. In one sense, our honeymoon was over. In another, it was just beginning.

33: JEANNE

BEFORE OUR WEDDING, John and I went through premarital counseling with an older couple who also served in Afghanistan and were mentors to us. One question was about our view of marriage. A communicator by nature and spiritual gifting, John filled several pages with his answer. I wrote one word.

John teased me for not completing my homework. Yet now he fully agrees that single word—*TEAM*—does sum up our marriage. We don't just love each other; we also share unity of vision and values. When it's hard or one of us lags, the other steps up alongside. Through the good and the bad, we stick together, knowing that breaking up our team isn't even an option because God brought us together.

On the day of our wedding, we may have known little about each other except that God had called us to be together. By the time we returned from those precious days of honeymoon, we'd become that team. We were excited to make our first home in Feyzabad instead of heading to the USA to start our marriage in American-style comfort and ease as some might have expected.

Our first home was indeed small and simple. It consisted of just two second-story rooms above our NGO office. Soon our wedding tushak had flattened out enough to provide space for both of us. Our other furnishings included a few pictures, some shelving, floor rugs, and additional tushaks for sitting. We also had a tiny kitchen area with a small cabinet and propane camp stove we used to make tea or simple meals.

Indoor plumbing consisted of a chamber pot to supplement the "squatty-potty" that was outside across the courtyard. Our only running water, as John jokingly described, was his dash with a bucket to the neighborhood tap or the compound's *jui*, Feyzabad's canal system that held water in rainy seasons. In contrast, thanks to the compound's solar panels and satellite system, we had far more reliable electric light and internet than I'd enjoyed in Kabul.

One other major lack was privacy. Students and staff came and left the compound all day. Even most of our meals were eaten with the Afghan staff, often prepared by the office cook in his courtyard kitchen. Any time of the day or night, a knock at the gate could herald a visitor, a crisis John had to deal with, or even a God-seeker with questions.

If this might seem a less-than-ideal start to marriage, it proved just the opposite. In part, because life itself in Feyzabad was slow-paced, and the scarcity of electricity throughout the town meant that our communal lifestyle ended after sunset. Unless some rare evening event or visit was scheduled, John and I had the compound to ourselves once darkness fell.

With no television or other distractions, this gave us long hours to be together. We'd sit outside, talking and praying. Other times we'd enjoy the peace and quiet, simply drinking in the sweet scent of roses and other flowers along with the brilliance of constellations against a night sky undimmed by man-made illumination.

Every day I found myself thanking God for letting us spend these first months of marriage in Afghanistan. If we'd gone back to the U.S. for this interval, we would have been pulled in different directions, flooded with people, travel, speaking engagements. We would not have had the focused time or peaceful solitude to cement our relationship, to develop the DNA of team, and to bond so closely as husband and wife.

Not that those months were devoid of socializing. One major difference in John's own daily life now that we were married was being able to visit as a couple acquaintances whose wives and extended family he'd never been introduced to as a single man. We received many invitations to the homes of city leaders and community elders.

I would be escorted to the women's quarters while John joined male family members in a separate hospitality room. It was a new opening into Feyzabad society for both of us. Since our NGO staff and students were mostly male, I especially enjoyed developing female friendships.

Though we were still newlyweds, I soon began to suspect a new blissful experience was about to be added to our happiness. One evening after the last staff member had left the compound, I expressed my intuitions: "John, I think I'm pregnant."

In the surprise and celebration that followed, I couldn't have known how quickly this bubbling joy would become our first bitter sorrow as a couple.

34: JOHN

"SWEETHEART, WHAT DO YOU mean? Are you sure? What do we do now?"

Not the brightest response to my bride's announcement. I knew babies were a natural outcome of a loving marriage, yet I'd assumed it would take longer. I shared Jeanne's excitement, but immediate worries went through my mind. Health care in Feyzabad was sketchy. I knew nothing about pregnancy, nor did Jeanne for that matter.

A first step would be to confirm the pregnancy. An Afghan acquaintance maintained a small pharmacy in the front of his house, which warranted him the title of *dokter* (doctor) though his medical training was less than basic. Seeking him out, I fumblingly tried to explain that I needed a pregnancy test, the necessary Dari vocabulary unfamiliar to me.

Older, gray-haired, the pharmacist had known me since my earliest days as an unmarried aid worker. By the time he'd gleaned what I wanted, he was grinning widely. He handed me a small box. "This is what you need."

I turned the box over in my hands, clueless as to what I was supposed to do with it since the printed instructions were in no language I could read. Laughing, my friend took the box and explained how to use it. Then he leaned in to say quietly, "The Green Book you read from at your wedding. Could you get me a whole box of them?"

Whether he was genuinely interested in reading God's Word or just wanted them to sell, I don't know. But his request was a reminder that God was (is) always working. Our Heavenly Father had His purposes even in this mundane commission of a husband for his wife. I didn't have such a quantity of Holy Bibles on hand, but let him know I'd try to fulfill his request.

By the time I handed Jeanne the pregnancy test, my initial shock had worn off. We were both elated when the test verified that Jeanne was indeed pregnant. So our devastation was correspondingly acute when within a few days Jeanne began experiencing severe abdominal pain. It didn't take long to realize she was suffering a miscarriage.

We called expat medical friends. Their professional advice was that there was nothing we could do. We'd just have to let nature take its course. Jeanne and I were both distraught when we hung up the phone. All night we clung together, praying, crying, and comforting each other. By morning our child was gone. Considering the short time we'd even known of our child's presence, the depth and pain of our grief was unanticipated.

In the morning I had to leave Jeanne home recovering to attend a meeting with a small group of Afghans. These were all men who had known me for several years as a single guy and had been at my wedding. They'd also all been married much longer than me. Sitting together with them for the first time as a married man created a fresh bond between all of us.

After the usual greetings, we began the meeting. I tried to keep all emotion from my tone and expression. But my companions knew me too well. One man broached the subject: "You are sad, John-Agha. What is wrong? Is it your family? Has there been bad news?"

I could see genuine concern on their faces. Fighting back tears, I explained briefly what had happened. In the culture where I'd been raised, men didn't burst into tears, especially in front of other men. Even more so in Afghan culture, where I'd hardly ever seen a grown man cry. But by the time I finished, I was stunned to see tears flowing down their faces.

"We are so sorry! We understand your experience. We know what you are feeling. All our mothers and wives have been through this!" was the gist of their response.

At that moment I realized these men did indeed understand exactly what Jeanne and I were going through. Afghanistan had one of the highest infant mortality rates in the world. Even more so in this isolated northeastern mountainous area with minimal health care where one in four children die in infancy and one in five mothers die in childbirth.

My companions were all husbands and fathers who had all endured the loss of loved ones. This was a part of their daily existence they'd never shared with a young, single American man who couldn't possibly understand their traumatic experiences. Now for the first time, I could truly empathize with the grief and pain that to them was an expected part of life.

We never returned to our planned discussion. Instead, we just sat together, crying, sharing, and consoling each other. Someone mentioned that the Holy

Book had a passage that talked about such comfort. I found it in my Dari New Testament, and we began to read it.

> Praise be to the God and Father of our Lord Jesus Christ, the Father of compassion and the God of all comfort, who comforts us in all our troubles, so that we can comfort those in any trouble with the comfort we ourselves receive from God.
> —2 Corinthians 1:3-4 NIV

A difficult experience became an incredibly poignant time of connection at a whole new depth with these Afghan friends. Another unusual experience also brought me comfort in this time and Jeanne as well when I told her about it. I don't have regular visions or vivid dreams I can remember in the morning. I've already mentioned a few exceptions—the vision of serving in Afghanistan and the dream about writing the book *Inside Afghanistan.*

The night after the miscarriage, Jeanne and I talked and prayed together as usual before drifting off to sleep. Sometime during the night, I had a dream. It remains crystal-clear in my memory. I was in heaven where I met a girl who told me her name was Elizabeth Dawn. She also said, "Daddy, I'm okay."

Although completely mystified by what I saw, I have absolute assurance she was the child we lost and that one day we will meet her again in heaven, our eternal home, the place Jesus Christ is preparing for us.

35: Jeanne

I FOUND A SENSE OF relief in the dream John shared with me. In contrast, I also had a dream after the miscarriage that was less comforting. In my dream, I was worshipping God in prayer, my hands raised in praise. But some unseen force bound my hands, then bound my mouth so I couldn't praise anymore. I knew the dream signified a spiritual attack.

Even before our marriage, John had been scheduled for a business trip and book-signing tour across Australia. I began praying that God would make this trip a second honeymoon for us, a mutual healing for our grief. With my dream in mind, I also told John I wanted to have our brothers and sisters in Christ we'd be visiting throughout Australia pray over us.

The trip exceeded my expectations. We spent a total of three weeks visiting Sydney, Melbourne, Brisbane, Perth, and other places. In Perth, we visited a church that had given generously to aid work in Afghanistan. The women's leadership took me aside, praying over me and over my womb. One leader shared a message the Holy Spirit had laid on her heart: "God is going to give you and John children and soon."

Spiritually, emotionally, and physically healed, we returned to Feyzabad renewed and refreshed. As my sister-in-Christ in Perth had prophesied, I was soon pregnant again. More so, John and I had grown closer together in our grief than in our happiness. *Team* indeed described the bond of unity with which we were learning to navigate hard times as well as good. A Bible passage written millennia ago by King Solomon took on special meaning for us:

> Two are better than one because they have a good return for their labor . . . If either of them falls down, one can help the other up . . . Though one may be overpowered, two can defend themselves. A cord of three strands is not quickly broken.
> —Ecclesiastes 4:9-12 NIV

God's Word always spoke to our situation. This was a daily blessing as my new pregnancy was far from the end of trying times facing us. Just a few weeks after we'd confirmed I was once again pregnant, John traveled to Kunduz. I was praising God that we'd now passed the stage at which I'd experienced my previous miscarriage and my pregnancy appeared to be going well. We'd already determined that we wanted our first child to be born in Afghanistan, just as we'd chosen to be married here. If not in Feyzabad, then in Kabul where I was born.

The first days of John's absence, I thought my growing fatigue and nausea was just morning sickness. Then I noticed the dark hue of my urine, a yellowing of my eyes and skin. I called an expat doctor friend, who came to give me a medical checkup. She informed me I'd contracted Hepatitis A.

A highly contagious virus, Hepatitis A affects the liver, hence the jaundice. It can be spread through contaminated food and water or through contact with someone or something already infected. It is especially prevalent in less-developed nations due to lack of hygiene and clean water. The good news was the illness didn't typically affect an unborn child. Mild cases generally petered out within a few weeks with no further treatment than rest and a careful diet.

When I called to tell John the diagnosis, he insisted to cut short his trip and come back home. I wasn't yet particularly worried. But within a few days, it became clear that what I had wasn't a mild case. I couldn't tell how much of the fatigue, nausea, abdominal and joint pain, along with a low-grade fever, was the hepatitis and how much was morning sickness. But I soon could keep no food down at all.

As I grew weaker, the decision was made to medivac me to the CURE Hospital on an outgoing UN flight. John accompanied me, and one of our NGO drivers picked us up at the Kabul Airport. Taking one look at me, the driver announced with alarm, "You have hepatitis!"

He was sincerely concerned. So were other former Afghan colleagues who'd been among those at my engagement party vowing to stand in *loco parentis* for me. They'd given their blessing for John-Agha to carry off their dearest Najiba-jaan to the far-off mountains of Feyzabad. Now within months I'd been returned seriously ill and jaundiced, and they weren't pleased at all. Several volunteered to donate blood if I needed a transfusion.

While touched by their concern, I felt too sick to think of anything except panic over what my condition might be doing to my unborn child. Since there was no real medical treatment, I was assigned to bedrest at a guesthouse near the hospital. John did his best to ply me with liquids and food, spoon-feeding me apple sauce and other easily digestible nourishment. But I could keep down little of either.

To complicate matters, I was also experiencing intermittent bleeding, so my illness was compounded by the fear of another miscarriage. Day by day, I could feel my body shutting down. Even finding strength to pray was increasingly difficult. One day I said weakly to John, "Is the room supposed to sway like a boat?"

Alarmed, he called the doctor. But there was nothing to be done except hope and pray that my body's own immune system would begin fighting back. Then one day in despair, the room spinning around me, I mustered up the energy to cry out to God: "Lord, either I am going to die soon and lose this baby too or you are going to heal me. But I can't go on like this!"

I didn't find out until later that on this very morning a female Brazilian colleague had stood up during our team prayer meeting to share a message God had given her: "Jeanne will be healed as God promises in Malachi, chapter four: 'But to you who fear My name, the Sun of Righteousness shall rise with healing in His wings.'"

What I did receive in response to my desperate plea was perfect peace that I was in God's loving hands no matter what happened. While my condition underwent no sudden change, bit by bit I began feeling better. One day I ate some caramelized popcorn, and it actually tasted good. By Christmas, three months into my pregnancy, I had improved enough for John and me to fly back to America to spend the holidays with our extended family there.

Simultaneously, my bleeding also stopped. While in the U.S., we took time to visit an obstetrician. The doctor ordered so many tests that we braced ourselves for bad news. Instead, he informed us that my pregnancy was progressing normally and the baby was in perfect health. This was also reassurance that it was God's will for me to give birth in Afghanistan. By the time we flew back to Feyzabad in mid-February, I felt healed again, though still quite fatigued for the rest of my pregnancy.

Three weeks before my due date, we traveled to Kabul to stay until the birth. At first we stayed at a guesthouse near our NGO office since John had some project work to complete. Our plan was to move closer to the hospital before my actual due date.

But on the day we'd scheduled our move, some American soldiers were involved in a deadly accident. This in turn led to a major riot with thousands of angry Afghans marching through Kabul, including the street that ran past our guesthouse. Armed with shovels, sticks, and iron bars, the mob was revengefully attacking and setting on fire anything they perceived to be foreign.

Not knowing about the riot, John and I headed out to the gate to hail a taxi. In God's mercy, the chowkidar stopped us just before we stepped out the gate into a street filled with raging protestors. He managed to whisk us back inside the guesthouse before anyone could possibly recognize us as foreigners.

We thanked God for His intervention and then continued praying for God to bring peace in the midst of chaos. By evening things had calmed down enough for us to leave. So we made the journey to the other side of the city, where we had made arrangements to stay at a guesthouse near the CURE Hospital until the birth of our child.

When I finally went into labor, there were no complications at all. Unusual in Afghanistan, John was with me in the delivery room. After the darkness of night, on a beautiful morning as the sun rose with brilliant light above Kabul's golden-brown mountain peaks, our first-born son, John Mack Weaver IV, arrived straight into his father's hands, a healthy 8 lbs., 3 ounces.

Our son's dawn arrival with bright rays of sunshine beaming all around was an unforgettable moment for us. A sense of God's presence and peace along with grateful praise overwhelmed us as John and I met our baby for the first time. Now we were not just a team of two, but of three.

36: JOHN

I AM NOT GOOD WITH BLOOD. I mean, *really* not good with even a glimpse of the red stuff. This is admittedly inconvenient for an aid worker in extremely dangerous and remote places.

So it was an uplifting experience that didn't at all hurt my self-esteem when I made it through my son's entire birth without passing out. The midwife, an expat friend, even allowed me to receive our first-born son and cut his umbilical cord.

This broke Afghan cultural norms, since husbands wouldn't normally be present during a birth. The majority of births here are not in hospitals at all, but at home under supervision of female family members and at best a local midwife. Factors that contribute to Afghanistan's high infant and mother mortality rates. So I was thankful to have trained medical care for my wife and son.

After the birth, we returned to the guesthouse where we'd been staying. Like the days following our wedding, Afghans and expats stopped by to see the child, congratulate me on a healthy son, and pray God's blessing over our family. Some Afghan friends asked when we'd be circumcising John Mack, a custom in Islam, Judaism, and among many Christians as well.

We'd already decided to follow the instructions God had given in the Holy Scriptures (Genesis 17:10; Leviticus 12:3; Luke 2:21; Philippians 3:5), so on the eighth day, Jeanne and I returned with our firstborn to the hospital. If husbands don't typically attend births in Afghanistan, a mother isn't normally present for male circumcision. So Jeanne stayed in the waiting room, spending her time in prayer for John Mack and the entire procedure.

In Afghanistan, just as in biblical times, circumcision is considered less a medical procedure than a religious ceremony. It is an act of faith or rite of passage, dedicating a son to be a follower of God. So Jeanne and I had agreed that I should remain at our son's side to read God's Word and pray over him while the Afghan doctor carried out the circumcision.

I did well as the doctor and nurse began initial preparations, praying aloud a succession of Bible passages and blessings, dedicating John Mack to the Lord God Almighty. Among my recitations was the Shema, one of Holy Scripture's earliest creeds or declarations of faith from the time of Moses and even quoted by Jesus the Messiah Himself:

Hear, O Israel: The Lord our God, the Lord is one.
—Deuteronomy 6:4-5 NIV

Love the Lord your God with all your heart and with all your soul and with all your mind and with all your strength.
—Mark 12: 29-30 NIV

Then suddenly John Mack cried out in anguish as the Afghan doctor reached the crucial part of the procedure. I'd heard my son cry several times since his birth when hungry or in need of a diaper change, but never in such piercing pain. Accompanying his scream was blood. No more than expected, but my own blood rushed to my head.

And that's all I remember until I opened my eyes to find myself stretched out on cold tile, water dripping from my face, and the nurse staring down at me.

37: JEANNE

I WAS PRAYING IN THE name of the Lord Jesus Christ as I kept an eye on the door separating me from my husband and newborn son. While I could neither see inside nor hear, I knew John was speaking Scripture over John Mack. I added my own heartfelt agreement as together we dedicated our son to the God of Abraham, Isaac, and Jacob.

We'd both been well-versed in what the procedure would entail, so I wasn't worried when I heard an infantile wail of pain and discomfort. Thankfully, the cries quickly subsided. A few minutes later, the nurse emerged with my son, who was still whimpering. She explained that breastfeeding him would be the best way to comfort him.

I was following her suggestion when I noted for the first time John's absence. It was some minutes before he staggered from the operating room, looking pale and oddly damp. The nurse explained what had happened. She'd tried to respond when John collapsed, but the doctor had directed, "First help me finish with the baby! The father will be just fine!"

John hadn't recovered consciousness until the nurse applied a generous sprinkling of water. While the incident admittedly had its humorous side, John's fall aggravated a prior back injury, and he was in far more pain than he let on to the hospital staff.

Currently the only healthy one of our little team, I carried off my sore and grumpy male family members for some well-earned rest and recovery.

38: JOHN

WITH THE BIRTH OF A healthy child and recovered fitness for both Jeanne and me, our time of trials and tribulations seemed to be over. Even better, our hopes of honoring God with a Christ-centered wedding and establishing a family of Christ-followers in Afghanistan had come to fruition more than we could have ever imagined. It never occurred to us that those factors would plunge us into a whole new set of challenges and troubles.

We were booked to fly Stateside in September 2006, less than three months after John Mack's birth. The trip included a full schedule of meetings and speaking engagements along with introducing our son to his extended family. Since we were still in Kabul, strolling down to the American Embassy with John Mack's birth certificate to apply for his U.S. passport seemed a simple next step. It proved anything but!

The first obstacle was that our son's Afghan birth certificate matched my own passport name, John Mack Weaver. His mother's passport was still in her maiden name, Jeanne Bonner. A situation we'd planned to deal with on our visit to America, since to apply for a new passport in Jeanne's new married name necessitated first having a certified wedding certificate. We'd had our friend Kurt, an ordained minister, perform our wedding specifically to avoid any complication on this issue.

We had also alerted the U.S. embassy in Kabul that two Americans were planning to get married in Afghanistan. No official objection had been raised to our plans, and at least one embassy-connected guest had been at our Kabul wedding. So it was a shock when they not only didn't approve John Mack's passport but refused to issue us a marriage certificate.

"To authenticate he is your legal son, you'll need to first show that you are legally married," I was told. "Since you were married in here, it's up to the Islamic Republic of Afghanistan to issue you an official wedding certificate."

Ratifying Kurt's ministerial credentials to perform our wedding should have been well within the U.S. consular agent's authority. But in 2006 the U.S. State Department was going the extra mile to accommodate the fledgling Karzai administration, so they were reluctant to intervene in any local bureaucratic process.

Another easy solution would have been to issue John Mack a passport in his mother's name as would be protocol for any single mother of American citizenship. But that would have implied a birth out of wedlock in a country where extramarital relations could be punishable by death from stoning.

In any case, Jeanne and I had committed from the beginning to submit ourselves wherever possible to Afghan culture and law. So I reluctantly conceded to applying for a wedding certificate through the Afghan court system. The complication was that our travel date was now less than two months away, not a long time span with Afghanistan's strict bureaucratic standards.

We asked our Afghan acquaintances, but none had any more idea of the procedure than we did. By their criteria, our very public double wedding was ample evidence we were legally married. We soon discovered there was no protocol in place for processing a wedding certificate for two foreigners—and Christ-followers at that.

Then an Afghan co-worker suggested we try the family court since typically it was the family court in one's locality that registered marriages. I took a taxi there. After a long wait in multiple lines, I was informed that I'd need to come back with seven witnesses who could testify they'd been at our wedding. Each would need a passport-sized picture for the documentation and must be willing to give both a verbal statement of witness and a thumbprint for ID.

This seemed simple enough. Just among our staff there were dozens who'd been at our wedding. I asked around to see who had time in their schedule to take passport pictures and accompany Jeanne and me back to the family court in Kabul.

Four men and three women quickly volunteered. Among the mix were expats, Pashtuns, and Tajiks. We stopped at a store to get passport photos for everyone. Then we headed to court, expecting to walk in, hand over the photos, testify to our wedding, give a few thumbprints, and walk out with official papers.

But before we'd even introduced our witnesses, some on the panel of family court judges were shaking their heads. Seven witnesses didn't mean just seven warm human bodies. I hadn't taken into account or had just forgotten that in Islamic law a woman only counted as half a witness in the court system. If we were going to include women, we'd need two for every male. More importantly, all the witnesses had to be local Afghans.

By this point I was so frustrated I'll admit to a totally unsanctified moment of irritability. Glaring back at the main judge who'd been speaking, I said, "Sir, are you saying your mother is only half a human being? Or that your wife and sisters are less of human beings than you are?"

This was one time when being an American proved an asset. Instead of an angry reprimand, I received pitying looks and some muffled chuckles. The judge I'd addressed spoke up calmly. "Well, I wouldn't say that. But it's the law, and there is nothing we can do about it."

Indeed there wasn't, so I conceded defeat and retreated to try again. This time I rounded up seven Afghan male guests from our wedding. Several of them were former mujahedeen, the tallest six feet, six inches. This time their credentials weren't questioned.

In turn, they testified, "I know John-Agha and his wife, Najiba-jaan. I personally witnessed their wedding." Each then proffered a photo and thumbprint. After a series of stamps and forms, I was finally handed a document signed by the family court judges that stated when and where Jeanne and I had been married.

I assumed we'd accomplished our goal. But when I returned to the American Embassy to apply for John Mack's passport, I was informed that because we were foreigners the local family court document had no validity. We'd need to have it authorized by the Ministry of Foreign Affairs as well as by the Ministry of Interior, which controlled all law enforcement and the judiciary.

So began an ongoing cycle of visiting government offices, standing in lines, and receiving—sometimes kindly, sometimes harshly—flat rejections to what had once seemed a simple request. By this time I was no longer bringing Jeanne and John Mack along. The waits were typically long, and there was nothing Jeanne could contribute to accelerate things. It was a frustrating, discouraging, even infuriating process, especially as we came closer and closer to our planned travel date.

It wasn't long before certain factors became clear to me. The first was the real reason we were being denied our needed documentation. Although the Taliban had been removed from power, the recently ratified constitution identified Afghanistan as an Islamic Republic under Sharia law with Islam its only officially recognized religion.

Just three months before our son's birth, a returning Afghan refugee who had become a Christ-follower during his exile had been arrested under the indictment of apostasy. While working behind the scenes to secure the man's release, the American Embassy had been reluctant to criticize in any way the new Afghan regime's human rights record.

With such a precedent, the Afghan judiciary was proving equally leery to take any action that would validate a Christ-centered ceremony. It didn't help that under Islamic Sharia law all judges were religious clerics.

To muddy the waters even further, my wife and son had both been born in here, so the judiciary could claim if they chose that Jeanne and John Mack were Afghan citizens for whom being a follower of Christ was illegal.

Overall, the court personnel were courteous. Yet they made it clear someone else would have to take the risk of endorsing the wedding of two Christ-followers on Afghan soil. Finally, one judge advised me bluntly, "Why don't you just get married again as Muslims? You are a man of faith who worships God as we do. All you've to do is recite the Shahada, signifying you've converted to Islam. Then you'll have no problem. We can sign any document you want."

Similar in form and purpose to the Shema, the Jewish declaration of faith, the Shahada in its shortest form states, "There is no god but Allah, and Muhammad is the messenger of Allah." The only official requirement for converting to Islam is to recite the Shahada publicly. The ritual isn't dissimilar to the confession of faith for Christ-followers in the book of Romans, chapter 10:

> If you declare with your mouth, "Jesus is Lord," and believe in your heart that God raised Him from the dead, you will be saved. For it is with your heart that you believe and are justified, and it is with your mouth that you profess your faith and are saved. As the Scripture says, "Anyone who believes in Him will never be put to shame." For there is no difference between Jew and Gentile—the same Lord who is Lord of all richly blesses all who call on Him. For "whoever calls on the name of Lord will be saved."
>
> —Romans 10:9-13 NIV

Of course, the judge's suggestion was out of the question—and not just because Jeanne and I are devout followers of the Lord Jesus Christ.

"I do love God with all my heart, mind, soul, and strength," I responded courteously. "But even to receive the official wedding documentation, I couldn't get married again because my wife has already borne me a son. Jesus Christ tells us that if a man even looks upon a woman with lust in his heart, he is committing adultery. To say we aren't lawfully married, yet already have a son, would be saying I am a liar and my wife is an immoral woman and that we've sinned against God. This would be completely shameful and displeasing to God."

The chatter among the judges made evident this was an argument they understood. One spoke up. "You claim Isa al-Masih has said that lust for a woman is akin to adultery. I have never heard that."

"Would you like to see it for yourself? It is in the Holy Book." I pulled a Dari New Testament from where I kept one tucked into my vest. Flipping the pages to the Sermon on the Mount in the Gospel according to Matthew, I showed it to the judge, who began reading aloud with clear interest:

> You have heard that it was said, "You shall not commit adultery." But I tell you that anyone who looks at a woman lustfully has already committed adultery with her in his heart.
> —Matthew 5:27-28 NIV

The Scripture generated more murmured conversation between the judges. Then they swiveled to address me. "These are good words. You are correct that to lust in one's heart is as sinful as adultery and that a real relationship with God is from the heart, not just an outward ritual of words. You've indeed shown yourself more God-fearing than we are."

Some of the judges showed signs of sympathy. But they also firmly stated that they couldn't give me the necessary documentation. "If you will not convert to Islam and marry again as Muslims, you will have to go to the Supreme Court. Only they have the authority to override the law."

I left disappointed, yet increasingly aware of why the Sovereign Lord had brought Jeanne and me to Afghanistan—to be salt and light—to advance God's Kingdom even in the most difficult places and times. Not just with these judges but over and over during this entire process, God was creating opportunities right in front of me to share His Holy Word.

Even the tedious taxi drives to and from government offices provided occasions to be a witness. When I entered a taxi I'd raise my hands, palms upward, to give thanks and pray for God's blessing, as would any devout Muslim. This typically led to questions, especially if the driver recognized me as a foreigner. Once I explained my current dilemma, I was repeatedly asked why I didn't just solve my problem by converting or perhaps paying a large bribe.

"Praise God, I'm a follower of Isa al-Masih," I would respond. Invariably this turned the driver's questions to spiritual issues, giving opportunity to explain what it meant to be a Christ-follower.

I am once again pursuing my bride, I recognized. *This time just trying to prove she IS my bride. Even through all this, Christ is also relentlessly pursuing His own bride, shining His light, revealing His love, and sowing seeds of faith as the Lord of the Harvest.*

Our final step was now in sight: an official certification of our family court documents by the Supreme Court of the Islamic Republic of Afghanistan. But what a step! I tried to get an appointment for a Supreme Court judge to even hear my case—all to no avail.

I knew friends and colleagues all over the country and beyond were praying for a resolution to our dilemma. I trusted that God had His purpose even in the continued delay. Still, my natural self was also disheartened, impatient, and a bit upset. I'd spent enough years navigating Afghan bureaucracy to know that I could be going around in circles indefinitely. By now I'd exhausted every local avenue for approving our wedding certificate. If the embassy remained adamant, I might be forced to consider acquiring a passport for John Mack by some less than ideal means.

As the Afghan proverb goes, walls have mice and mice have ears. News of our wedding had already spread. Now the love story of this foreign couple committed to the Afghan people enough to not only get married here but bring their firstborn son into the world on Afghan soil was becoming known as well. We found out that a few of the judges and others we'd interacted with were persons of peace and seekers of truth. By now, our stubborn perseverance as I made my rounds day after day to various locations began to generate more interest and empathy even as my pleas continued to be rejected.

One day, fatigued from going from office to office, I ran into one of the female judges from the family court. After the usual greetings, she stepped aside to tell me quietly, "I'm so sorry that I can't help you. But I have an acquaintance who is a judge at the Supreme Court. If you can be there tomorrow morning at 10 a.m., he might be able to help you. Just give this name to the reception clerk."

Wow! This development could only have come through divine intervention. Immediately I sent out a request to friends and family to be praying with Jeanne and me the next morning at 10 a.m. Before the hour, I presented myself at the gate to the Supreme Court compound. The guards quickly informed me that I wasn't on their list of authorized visitors.

"Look, I'm supposed to be meeting with this judge," I pleaded. "I need to be inside by 10 a.m. Please, I can't express strongly enough how important this is. If I miss this appointment, I'll be in real trouble."

An American who looked like an Afghan and spoke Dari was unusual enough to gain me a further hearing. The guards expressed sympathy at my plight, but not enough to contravene their orders.

"I'm sorry, but we can't let you in because the court is now in session," I was informed. "And the judge you wish to see is probably in session too, so he wouldn't be available to see you. You'll just have to come back another day and with the proper authorization."

Either to make me feel better or just being good Afghans, the guards invited me to join them for a cup of tea. I had no intention of leaving until I saw the judge, so I accepted the offer. We were chatting amicably when I noticed a man emerging from the courthouse. I recognized him as one of the many officials I'd dealt with during this bureaucratic ordeal. He recognized me as well and headed over to join us.

"What are you doing here, John-Agha?" he asked.

I displayed my now rather well-worn documents. "Judge So-and-So—" I gave the name of the official who'd sent me here. "—told me to be here at 10 a.m. to present my case to this Supreme Court Judge."

"Then what are you waiting for?" the man cut in with a smile. "Come! I'll take you to him myself."

The next thing I knew, I was being led past the security checkpoint. This time I wasn't given the runaround or just ushered to the reception area where other supplicants were waiting to be seen. At just the right moment, God had parted the seas and I was being led straight through to the first area of the Supreme Court. A few minutes later, I was being introduced to the judge I'd come here to see.

My companion quickly explained who I was and the mutual friend/judge who had sent me. His sympathy towards my situation was clear as he concluded, "This man is a guest in our country, a friend to the Afghan people. He has all the documents he needs, and there is no reason why they shouldn't be signed. Please help the man and his family."

I have no idea how much the judge knew about my situation or the reasons for past delays. But he listened respectfully and then got on the phone to the office of the chief justice of the Supreme Court. Within a short interval, a clerk came in to collect my documents. I learned later that he'd taken them directly into the Supreme Court chambers where the chief justice immediately signed them. Once they were officially stamped, I was led off to register the documents in a huge hand-written ledger.

After all the difficulties and delays, just like that, it was done! Two more stops were necessary to record the certified documents at the Ministry of Foreign Affairs and Ministry of Interior. Since the seal now stamped on them was the highest legal authorization in Afghanistan, we were given no further trouble.

Soon, I returned to the American Embassy with an official Afghan wedding certificate confirming that John Weaver and Jeanne Bonner, both citizens of the United States of America, were legally married in the Islamic Republic of Afghanistan.

Now that we were verified as the lawfully married parents of John Mack Weaver IV, a birth certificate and his passport were quickly granted. When our scheduled flight stateside lifted off from Kabul International Airport, all three of us were aboard.

In God's perfect timing and in such a way that could be only divine intervention, God Almighty had answered our prayers. Now my ties to this ancient land that had become my home included both a wife and a son whose passports listed Afghanistan as their place of birth.

39: JEANNE

WE RETURNED FEELING THAT our lives had come full circle. Both John and I had come to Afghanistan single. Now we were not only a married couple, but parents. Since family is paramount in the Afghan culture, this new dynamic opened more doors within Afghan society not accessible to us as young, single adults.

Our first Christmas as a married couple had been celebrated in the U.S., our pleasure at seeing family and friends punctuated with anxiety about my pregnancy and recovery from hepatitis. So celebrating John Mack's first Christmas and our second as a married couple in the home we had made together in Feyzabad held special joy for us.

With all the bustle of daily responsibilities and family life, we never lost sight of God's ultimate purpose for sending us to Afghanistan—to be witnesses of His redeeming love to the Afghan people in both word and deed. The holiday festivities provided many opportunities to share the true meaning of Christmas—the miracle and mystery of the incarnation:

> The angel of the Lord stood before them, and the glory of the Lord shone around them. Then the angel said, "Don't be afraid, I bring you *good news* of great joy that will be for all people. Today in Bethlehem, the

city of King David, a Savior has been born for you; He is Christ the Lord. This will be a sign: you will find a baby wrapped in cloths and lying in a manger." Suddenly there appeared with the angel a multitude of heavenly host praising God and saying, "Glory to God in the highest and on earth peace, goodwill toward men!"

—Adapted from Luke 2:9-14

The choice of a name is as significant in Afghan culture as in biblical times. The name we'd chosen for our firstborn allowed us to explain how John Mack was named after John the Baptist (Yaiyah), a prophet known by Muslims as well as Christians. This explanation would lead to the role of John the Baptist as the forerunner sent to prepare the way and proclaim the coming of the Messiah, the perfect Lamb of God whose atoning sacrifice would take away the sins of the world (Luke 1:13-17; John 1:19-34).

By now we were realizing that we needed more space as a growing family than our two-room makeshift apartment above the NGO office. Above all, it was really challenging to receive female visitors with their children in a compound overrun most days by male staff and students. In March 2007, we moved into a small house overlooking the Kokcha River.

Our immediate neighbor was also our landlord. A mud wall separated our smaller courtyard from his. This small, two-story residence was divided into two rooms downstairs and two upstairs. The upstairs became our living quarters with the downstairs as receiving salons for either male or female visitors. For light, we had a few bulbs that ran off local generator powered electricity from 7-9 p.m., along with plenty of candles and flashlights.

Heat for the winter consisted of barrel-shaped wood-burning stoves made of metal. Propane gas was becoming more available, so we eventually acquired some gas heaters as well. Like our prior apartment, there was no running water, so we depended on the *jui* when it held water or brought it in from the river or neighborhood spigot.

I loved my new home with its tranquil greenness and the placid waters of the Kokcha River rolling past. My daily life now centered on caring for my growing son, Yaiyah as the Afghans called him, and providing an oasis for my husband when he returned from the busy NGO office, a project trip, or spiritual journey.

Welcoming Afghan and expat women and children into our home was something else I enjoyed. But the tasks of cleaning, cooking, and washing took far more time without modern appliances, grocery stores, or refrigeration. Thankfully, our gray-haired chowkidar, Koko, helped me with some daily chores and errands.

Yet I hadn't realized how housebound my life had become until we heard that John's reputation had grown in the community as a God-fearing family man who kept his wife at home and bearing children. The gate to our immediate neighbors, the landlord's house, was almost always open. But for security reasons we kept our front gate locked, which led to an episode that only reinforced the gossip.

One morning when John left for work, he automatically locked the gate behind him. He'd forgotten that our chowkidar had the day off so he wouldn't be available to unlock the gate for guests. I myself didn't have a key, since typically John or the chowkidar was always there. As it happened, John had left just minutes before several neighbor women stopped by for a visit.

Hearing their persistent knocking, I headed down to the gate. Our gate had no slot or window through which I could make eye contact with my visitors. So all I could do was call out: "I'm so sorry. I cannot let you in because the gate is locked and Mr. John has taken the key!"

My situation wasn't as dire as it might sound since in any emergency I could have exited through our landlord's courtyard. But it didn't take long for the news to circulate that John-Agha was such a strict husband that he kept his wife Najiba-jaan locked inside the house when he was absent. A misunderstanding that increased local respect for this Christ-centered marriage!

John had reason to be protective of his family. Security was indeed a growing concern. By 2007, the resurgence of radical Islamic elements had escalated sharply from the year before. So-named "security incidents"— attacks on international military, contractors, national police posts, government offices and aid workers, as well as suicide bombings and IEDs (improvised explosive devices)—had drastically increased.

Unfortunately, the majority of casualties were Afghan civilians. But we couldn't ignore a rising hostility directed towards even those expatriates whose work—whether emergency relief, medical, educational, or community development—brought great benefit to the Afghan population.

In July 2007, a group of South Korean aid volunteers were kidnapped by the Taliban. Two of their male team members were executed before the others were released. Over the following months and years, a number of humanitarian workers, many from Christian organizations, would receive death threats, be kidnapped or even martyred.

We lived in the Northern Alliance area where the Taliban had never taken control. So we trusted optimistically that the good will our NGO had accrued for its service and John's own strong personal relationships with local leaders would provide its own protection. I'd come to love my new life in this remote area as much as John did. This was home. We were now joyously expecting a second child and had even discussed remaining in Feyzabad for the birth since all had gone so well with the first birth.

Still, we'd slowly begun to recognize a change in the atmosphere, especially towards John. He was now being called the "Christian mullah." Nor had the events of our wedding been forgotten. Those who'd expressed anger then continued to agitate, and the resurgence of Taliban extremism across Afghanistan gave them new allies. We learned that the religious leaders were using Friday services at the mosque to stir up hostility towards the foreign presence. At times they even preached against John over the loudspeakers.

Finally, some of John's closest Afghan friends informed him bluntly, "John-Agha, because of the good projects you do for our people, we speak up for you. When you speak of your faith in Isa al-Masih, however, we cannot defend you. You have been a trusted friend, honorable leader, and faithful servant to our people. But there are those who wish to harm you. For the sake of your family and for us as your friends, it is best you move to some other place where you aren't so well-known."

40: JOHN

I DIDN'T WANT TO WORRY Jeanne with the reality that the rumors were not just of growing hostility, but actual death threats. I shouldn't have been surprised. Whenever God begins to work, the devil and those opposed to the advancement of Christ's Kingdom will strike back. And God's Spirit was moving in Feyzabad, throughout Badakhshan, and other areas too.

Then I was approached with a new opportunity. Our NGO country director Georg was relocating from Kabul back to Germany. Would I be willing to take his place? As Jeanne and I spent time praying, fasting, and heart-searching over this request, we both began to realize that God was sovereignly orchestrating this unforeseen development.

It wasn't just because Feyzabad had become a potential danger zone for us as well as for our friends, whose association with the "Christian mullah" could place their lives in jeopardy too. God was offering us an opportunity to serve the Afghan people on a wider scale. Being based in the capital could allow us to have a bigger impact and greater influence. The idea of living in the big city no longer seemed so daunting to a country boy like me because I'd be there with Jeanne. And we both had many friends there now.

Our original plan was to move directly to Kabul. But as we continued to pray and seek God, we believed God was leading us to return to the U.S. for the birth of our second child. With tears, I said my goodbyes to Afghan friends with whom I'd worked through thick and thin, war and peace, for the last seven years. I kept my explanation simple.

"I thank God for sending me here to serve some seven years ago. Najiba-jaan and I were also greatly honored that you permitted us to hold our wedding in your city. And it was a great blessing for our son Yaiyah to be born in your country. But now it is time to honor our own parents by returning to America so they can be present for the birth of our second child."

This explanation made perfect sense to our family-oriented Afghan friends and neighbors. While they expressed sorrow at seeing us leave, their visible relief confirmed we were making the right decision.

Our second son, James Isaac, was born February 2008 in northern Virginia, not too far from where I was born in 1970. He was named after Jeanne's father. But his Afghan name would be his middle name, Isaac (Eshaq), the son born of God's promise to the patriarch Abraham and his wife Sarah.

As with our firstborn, named after John the Baptist, our second child's name carried significance for our Afghan acquaintances since Isaac is known as a prophet of righteousness and symbol of obedience and sacrifice to Almighty God. Every time we mentioned his name, we'd also be sharing Isaac's foreshadowing of the promised Messiah's own obedient offering as the sinless Lamb of God who willingly gave His life on the cross as the perfect sacrifice to take away the sins of the world.

41: JOHN

OUR MONTHS IN THE U.S. provided an easy transition for returning straight to Kabul instead of Feyzabad. For the next several years, the big city became our home base as I oversaw multiple teams of expats and Afghans carrying out humanitarian projects and various ministry initiatives across the country. A dear Afghan widow lady served as nanny to our children, so Jeanne was able to contribute her own skills in accounting and computer technology at our office.

God also gave us a third son, Joseph, or Yusuf, as they say in the Middle East. The eleventh son of the patriarch Jacob who saved God's people in Egypt and the earthly father of Jesus are two well-known men who share his name. The other Joseph in the Bible was the Jewish elder who had helped take the crucified body of Jesus Christ to his own tomb according to the prophecy and promise that the Messiah would rise again from the dead on the third day.

Though I counted it a privilege to be our NGO country director, it became progressively obvious my gifts and skill set were not in administration. I longed to focus more on leadership development and specialized training. Stretched beyond my capacity, I was nearing burnout because of the demanding workload, daily pressure, and high stress of life in Kabul.

There were also other challenges, spiritual opposition, and threats. Throughout these years, the security situation had continued to deteriorate. We'd lost many friends, both expat and Afghan, either due to kidnappings, forced evacuations, or targeted attacks. Slowly but surely, I began to realize the need to transition on to another season of life.

In the fall of 2010, we found ourselves expecting our fourth child. With the growing needs of our family, increased stress and threats, along with Jeanne's pregnancy, I knew it was God's time to resign as country director and return to America for a longer break.

Over the next seventeen months, I enrolled in the John Maxwell Team certification program, took doctoral classes in leadership, and served as an interim school principal. In April 2011, our precious daughter, Joy Louise, joined our family. She has indeed been a bundle of joy to all of us.

When God sent us back to Afghanistan in 2012, it was to Herat, a Farsi-speaking-majority city near the western border with Iran. Dubbed the "Garden City," Herat is set in the fertile plain of the Hari River, known especially for its vineyards. Despite some war damage and modern construction, it remains filled with green parks, historical structures, and ruins dating all the way back to Alexander the Great when Herat was a district capital of the Persian Empire.

Interestingly, one area in the province of Herat is named Injil, which means "Gospel" or "Good News." Perhaps it is because of the presence of Christ-followers many centuries ago. Because of our devotion to our

Savior's life-giving message, we gave our daughter Joy the name Injila, the female version of Injil. We'd chosen each of our children's names, both in English and Dari, to help convey the greatest love story of all. Now Team Weaver included John-Agha, Najiba, Yaiyah, Eshaq, Yusuf, and Injila.

Even though I still traveled some, my responsibilities of teaching and training proved far less stressful than the administration of an entire country operation. With my new role in leadership development, we settled into the house God provided, and Herat became home to the six of us. Sadly, any hope that the security situation would improve with our move lasted only about a year.

In September 2013, a Taliban force struck the American Consulate in Herat, detonating two car bombs along with a gun battle that killed several Afghan security officials. The Afghan presidential elections in April 2014 touched off a spate of riots and violence across the country. Then the Taliban attacked the Indian Embassy in Herat, resulting in another gun battle that lasted for hours.

The sounds of rapid gunfire and rocket-propelled grenades became commonplace as Taliban forces continued to attack government offices and police posts. The largest number of casualties remained Afghan law enforcement and civilians, not even counting assassinations of various prominent politicians and attacks on international military targets around the country. All of this left the expat humanitarian community feeling very much under siege.

Then in April 2014, the CURE Hospital in Kabul, where our first son was born, came under attack by one of the security guards assigned to protect its personnel. Among three Americans killed was a fellow colleague, also named John, and our friend Dr. Jerry Umanos, a gracious man who'd dedicated his life for almost a decade to bringing better medical care to the Afghan people. He'd also served as our pediatrician during our years in Kabul.

Of all the senseless deaths, this one hit us hard. Since I was known to have good language skills and cultural understanding, I was asked to lead a crisis debriefing for local Afghans who were also close to John Gable and Dr. Jerry.

It was a difficult, emotional experience as I facilitated the debriefing, walking through the details of their tragic death. Together, we cried, listened to one another, and shared stories about John and Dr. Jerry. We also gave thanks to God for their godly lives, precious memories, positive impact, and enduring legacy.

I spoke about their faith as well as the blessed assurance and living hope of eternal life in heaven, the place Isa al-Masih had prepared for them. Dr. Jerry's wife had already given a TV interview, speaking of the love she and her husband had for the Afghan people and how she'd forgiven the shooter because of the grace and mercy of their Savior, Jesus Christ.

Together, Afghan and expat, Christian and Muslim, we prayed, lighting candles in remembrance of John Gable, Dr. Jerry, and others we knew who'd sacrificed their lives in service to the Afghan people.

42: JEANNE

EVEN WHILE WE GRIEVED over the loss of friends and colleagues, we couldn't be angry with the Afghan people. One decision we'd made while still living in Kabul was to exercise sensible security precautions while also refusing to live in fear. We were situated in a neighborhood that was largely Afghan. Dressing and living in community as they did, we didn't stand out obviously as foreigners. We felt surrounded by Afghan colleagues, neighbors, and friends we trusted.

Most Afghans were as appalled as we were by the violence. Often when bad news came, whether in Feyzabad, Kabul, or Herat, Afghan co-workers, friends, or neighbors would express their disdain, grief, and pain over atrocities committed by evil extremists. They would also remind us that such wicked acts of terrorism were not representative of their faith.

Still, as the situation worsened, it was difficult not to cast a suspicious eye on some Afghans or worry whether security officers might not be renegades like those who'd turned on Dr. Jerry. When the American Consulate in Herat was bombed, the explosion and subsequent gun battle could be heard from our house. Over the following months, clashes between Afghan security forces and insurgents became more common.

Since our children could also hear the gunfire, we had to give them some explanation. We'd often say that the police were going after bad guys, so we'd have to stay inside until they were finished. Then we'd pray together.

We did our best to shield our children from the reality that sometimes foreigners like us were being targeted. Regularly, we'd put on a children's movie or praise-and-worship music to drown out the noise or so that John and I could pray and talk privately. Especially for me and the children, we were beginning to feel like hostages in our own home.

In July, we had a respite from the tension when we flew to Dubai for a retreat. The immediate sense of relaxation and safety we felt, not just as adults but our children, underscored just how much stress we'd been living under. For a few days at least, our children could freely play outdoors, ride bikes, swim in a pool, laugh loudly, and sing with the carefreeness and lightheartedness that should be a child's birthright. We returned to Herat rested and renewed, ready to get back to work.

As we took a taxi home from the airport, the driver informed us that another expat had been killed that morning. He was speaking Dari, and our four children in the back seat were making enough noise they didn't catch what he'd said. John asked the driver a few questions and then started praying. Tears were already welling up in my eyes as my mind raced to think who among the small international community was currently in town.

We soon learned the victims were two dear Finnish ladies who worked for another aid organization. The report was that they'd been gunned down by men on a motorcycle while taking a taxi to the bazaar. Again our hearts were broken.

If we'd felt under siege before, now we were advised to not even set foot outside our compound. John did go out when asked to meet with the staff of our two slain Finnish friends as well as to teach some evening leadership classes. Otherwise, we remained on lockdown for the next forty-five days. Many NGOs began to evacuate expatriate personnel and even reposition senior Afghan staff.

We reminded ourselves that the Afghan people were suffering far more than we were. Anyone with a government position was being targeted—judges, police officers, school teachers, city officials. Even some of our neighbors were staying inside due to similar threats. Whether related to the brewing hostility towards foreigners, the wide-spread accusations of election fraud, or the Taliban simply using that as an excuse, Herat along with other places remained in upheaval with insurgent attacks and suicide bombings at an all-time high.

By fall of 2014, through prayer and counsel, we recognized God was bringing our season in Herat to a close. Our plan was to transition back to Kabul, where John could pursue a countrywide focus on leadership development. Since we'd already scheduled a trip to spend Christmas with our parents, we packed up our personal items and sent several boxes to be stored in

Kabul. Then we spent several days receiving friends, colleagues, students, and neighbors before boarding a plane to the U.S.

Just days after our arrival, we received the worst news of all. A colleague and his two teenage children, along with two Afghans, were killed in a Taliban attack at their house in Kabul only a few blocks from where we'd planned to move in 2015.

Such targeted killings affected every NGO and their personnel. Many expats were either asked to leave the country or chose on their own to relocate. When our NGO made the official decision to evacuate any remaining foreign staff, we were still on our winter break in America.

After seeking God's will and discussing with our leaders and mentors, we made the decision for John to return to Afghanistan to resume the spring leadership classes. He would also check out the possibility of relocating our family in Kabul or to another location.

Then the day before John's departure, I learned to my surprise that I was pregnant. Birthing our fifth child at age forty-three was unplanned!

43: JOHN

THIS WAS A HARD TRIP for me—possibly the hardest. Although alone for the first time since 2005, I was grateful to be inside Afghanistan because there were friends and co-workers to see and much to do. Yet learning that Jeanne was unexpectedly pregnant with our fifth child brought home the realization that I was not just taking myself back into a conflict zone of escalating danger, but our growing family, who had their own spiritual, emotional, and physical needs.

Yes, I was willing to lay down my life, but I was also a husband, father, leader of Team Weaver. What was God saying to me? What was God's will—not just for my life, but for the family God had given me?

The decision facing me was both extremely difficult and painful. Not once had Jeanne and I considered that this furlough, like all the others, wouldn't end with a trip back to the land of our calling. Ever since God had first placed me inside Afghanistan in 2000, I'd embraced the long-term commitment of serving there.

Now, through wise counsel and the Holy Spirit speaking to my heart, God was making it clear that at least for the present we were not to return. But if not Afghanistan, then where? What was God leading us to next?

44: JEANNE

JOHN RETURNED FROM HIS spring trip to Afghanistan heartbroken and tearful. Grieving together, we accepted that for now the door was closed for us to go back as a family.

We'd been staying at my parents' home near Washington, D.C. They would have loved for us to remain there as we welcomed our fifth child. But as we prayed for guidance, God opened the door for us to move to Oklahoma. In His faithfulness and goodness, God provided a house for us, several ministry opportunities, and most of all a community.

The semi-rural setting was as distant from the turmoil we'd left behind as day is from night. I wondered at times just why God had taken us to a place so different from any place I or John had ever lived. Yet as the weeks passed, I recognized God met a need our family had lacked—a sense of security and stability.

We couldn't have found a more peaceful environment than our new home in Oklahoma. And just how much we needed it became evident as John and I, along with our four children, now ages four through eight years old, slowly recovered from the stress of living in a constant war zone.

45: JOHN

WHEN WE RETURNED TO the USA, Jeanne and I had a time of debriefing with a counselor. Part of this involved acknowledging that, as much as we loved Afghanistan and were called by God to serve the Afghan people, the stressful and traumatic events of the last several years had left us battling some degree of PTSD (post-traumatic stress disorder). We also needed help grieving our losses and processing our experiences in order to hear God's voice and discern His will during this transitional time.

By the birth of our fifth child, Judah, named after the fourth son of Jacob whose lineage produced the promised Messiah (Genesis 49:10; Micah 5:2; Revelation 5:5), also called the Lion of the Tribe of Judah, God had given us some answers about this new unplanned season.

Beyond the thirty-three-plus million Afghans living inside Afghanistan, five million more have scattered outside the country. Some have returned over the years since 9/11, but the heightened insurgency of the Taliban and ISIS has led to a resurgence of Afghans seeking refugee status. There are also thousands of Afghans studying abroad, some of whom are our former co-workers or students.

So what does the life and ministry of Team Weaver look like today? Jeanne continues to be a wonderful wife, an amazing full-time mom, and a creative homeschool teacher. She is also involved in some other ministry initiatives.

Through global connections and strategic partnerships, I continue to use my experience, language ability, and cultural skills from our current base in the U.S., directly and via digital communication and social media. Several times a year, I travel back to Afghanistan and to other countries where Afghans have scattered as well as locations within the U.S.

My role still involves leadership development and specialized training. I also provide advocacy for the Afghan people, share resources, speak at conferences, teach at various venues, as well as coach and/or mentor a number of leaders and teams. Just as moving to Kabul didn't keep us from serving the people of Feyzabad, but expanded our influence throughout the country, being based outside of Afghanistan has opened more ways to assist the Afghan people.

We also love serving and interacting with international students and immigrants, especially Afghans. One of my former leadership students invited us to his wedding in Virginia, not too far from where I grew up. It seemed strange to attend an Afghan wedding in the USA, especially since our own wedding was in Afghanistan. But what a joy it was to celebrate with this friend as he received his bride.

Recently, some friends connected us to a new Afghan refugee family who'd just arrived. We reached out to help them resettle, just as we'd want someone to do for us and actually have experienced several times when we had to move. Knowing how disoriented and lost they must be feeling in a strange place with no relatives around, I took them several places to get furniture and supplies for their unfurnished apartment. When I learned they had three children close in age to ours, I asked our own young tribe if they would like to help welcome this family to America.

Thankfully, our children have many good memories of the Afghan people to balance all the conflict and challenges we experienced living in Afghanistan. Our kids were immediately excited to meet new Afghan friends. Accompanying me to the store, they carefully picked out a few toys, coloring books, crayons, pencils, and other supplies to give to each of the family's three children.

One of my sons wanted to buy the family a Holy Bible. I explained that might not be best on a first visit. But to remind them of the greatest love story of all, we did pick some children's books whose narratives would be familiar to them: Adam and Eve, Noah, Abraham, Moses, David, and even the birth of Christ.

The Afghan family was as overjoyed at friendly guests speaking their language as at the gifts we brought, especially when our children introduced themselves by their Afghan names. The mother exclaimed delightedly over our second son, James Isaac. "Your Eshaq (Isaac) looks and sounds like one of my nephews!"

We settled in over a cup of tea while the family shared just how much they were missing their homeland. It was a reminder that while we are physically outside of the land of the Afghans, it will never be absent from us. Our hearts will always be inside Afghanistan.

EPILOGUE

IT STILL AMAZES ME HOW I met my princess bride at her birthplace. Even after God caused our paths to cross in Kabul, we faced many challenges and cultural issues if we were to pursue a relationship or even enjoy meaningful communication in such a strict context.

Similarly, Jesus Christ is pursuing His Bride among every Afghan tribe. To do so, the Spirit of God and the Word of God have to overcome many societal barriers and spiritual strongholds. Just as it wasn't easy for Jeanne and me to find the appropriate place or time to be together, followers of Christ in Afghanistan have no freedom of worship or local church buildings. They gather in their homes, at a park, or even in their vehicles. Believers continue to face many dangers and difficulties even in other countries where they've migrated.

But despite what seems insurmountable, God is always at work. Yes, our gracious Father is hearing and answering prayer. Many are searching for answers they have not yet found.

How can we overcome hatred and revenge? How can we truly know God and experience His love? How can we be forgiven, have our shame covered, and our sins removed? How can we find lasting peace? How can we be delivered from the fear of death and know for sure we will go to Heaven to be with God when we die?

Afghans are hungry for the bread of life. They are thirsty for the living water Isa al-Masih promised. Dissatisfied and disillusioned, millions are yearning to discover the greatest love story of all: the reality of the Good News the Holy Bible describes in the Gospel according to John:

> For God so loved the world that He gave His only begotten Son, that whoever believes in Him should not perish but have everlasting life. For God did not send His Son into the world to condemn the world, but that the world through Him might be saved.
>
> —John 3:16-17 NKJV

Where will this life-changing love story take us? Ultimately, to the celestial place Jesus is preparing for all who follow Him as the Way, the Truth, and the Life (John 14:1-6). But while we are still here on earth, only our Everlasting Father fully knows. More than 2,500 years ago, God spoke this promise through the prophet

Jeremiah, which is written for our instruction in the Holy
Scriptures:

> For I know the thoughts that I think toward
> you, says the Lord, thoughts of peace and not of
> evil, to give you a future and a hope. Then you will
> call upon Me and go and pray to Me, and I will
> listen to you. And you will seek Me and find Me,
> when you search for Me with all your heart. I will
> be found by you, says the Lord.
> —Jeremiah 29:11-13 NKJV

We know our Heavenly Father's plans are good, not
just for us, but for the Afghan people. We continue to ask
God to bring blessings, revelation, salvation, and peace
to the land of the Afghans. We pray that Afghans will be
drawn to God's light and turn to Him wholeheartedly.
Whether they live inside Afghanistan or outside its
borders, may they know that God loves them and longs
to be found by them.

As Team Weaver, we hope that someday we may
return as a family to where Jeanne and I became
husband and wife, the country of her birth and John
Mack's too. Until then, we count it an honor and privilege
to continue serving and sharing with Afghans scattered
all around the globe.

For now, let us end where it all began—with God in
the beginning. Out of the abundance of His infinite love,
God fashioned man in His own image to enjoy His
presence and the beauty of all His creation. But though
the first man, Adam, had constant fellowship and a

perfect relationship with his Creator, it was not good for him to be alone without a human companion. Therefore, with intimate detail, God designed the first woman, Eve, as a suitable helper for Adam.

So God wrote the first human love story that hundreds of generations later would lead to our story as God brought Jeanne and me together. And in the fullness of God's own timing, we will one day see the triumphant culmination of all human history when the Beloved Bridegroom gloriously returns for His Bride, who will sing, "You are worthy...for You were slain, and have redeemed us to God by Your blood out of every tribe and tongue and people and nation" (Revelation 5:9). This rapturous reunion will also fulfill God's Word:

> Christ also loved the church and gave Himself for her, that He might sanctify and cleanse her with the washing of water by the word, that He might present her to Himself a glorious church.
> —Ephesians 5:25-27 NKJV

Yes, when the victorious King Jesus comes again with all honor, power, and splendor, there will be a great wedding feast, the marriage supper of the Lamb (Revelation 19:6-9). God's Word does not leave us in doubt, but has given us full assurance of just how **His-Story**—the greatest love story of all—will majestically climax:

> I saw a new heaven and a new earth, for the first heaven and the first earth had passed away...I saw the

holy city, New Jerusalem, coming down out of heaven from God, prepared as a bride adorned for her husband. And I heard a loud voice from heaven saying, "Behold, the tabernacle of God is with men, and He will dwell with them, and they shall be His people. God Himself will be with them and be their God. And God will wipe away every tear from their eyes; there shall be no more death, nor sorrow, nor crying. There shall be no more pain, for the former things have passed away." Then He who sat on the throne said, "Behold, I make all things new." And He said..."Write, for these words true and faithful."

—Revelation 21:2-5 NKJV

Amen! Even so come, Lord Jesus!

Also Available on Amazon:

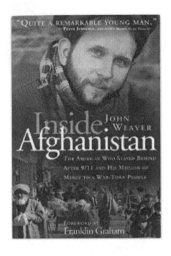

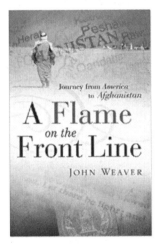

To learn more, please visit:

amazon.com/author/weaverunited
facebook.com/weaverunited
instagram.com/weaverunited
twitter.com/weaverunited

Made in the USA
Middletown, DE
03 May 2019